Ms. Kay and I have been a part of God's Forever Family with Mac and Mary for many years. Their incredible story began before we met them, but we are proud to have been a part of God's plan to raise them up and use them so mightily. This book shows the power of God when humble men and women choose to surrender their lives to Him. The Robertsons and Owens are cut from the same cloth—the servant towel of Jesus!

– Phil Robertson
The Duck Commander from *Duck Dynasty*

NEVER

LET

GO

MAC & MARY OWEN

with Travis Thrasher

LUCAS LANE

Never Let Go

Published by Lucas Lane Publishers
Batavia, Illinois
Mars Hill, North Carolina

LB Norton, editor
Erin Smith, copyeditor
Alyssa E. Force, designer

Cover photo: iStockPhoto LP
Author photo: Sheena Harper Photography

Printed in the United States of America
First Edition 2013
10 9 8 7 6 5 4 3 2 1

Library of Congress Cataloging-in-Publication Data
Owen, Mac, 1958–
Never let go: God's story of healing hurting lives/Mac and Mary Owen.
p. cm.
ISBN 978-0-9837726-0-6

To our three miracles:
Heath, Cherry, and Callie

And to our parents:
Alton & Jean Howard and Joe & Carla Owen,
who never stopped praying

FOREWORD

I am the founder of Celebrate Recovery, which began in 1991 at Saddleback Church in Lake Forest, California. Celebrate Recovery is a Christ-centered recovery ministry that is based on 8 Principles that are found in the Beatitudes in the Bible.

My wife, Cheryl, and I met Mac and Mary at the Celebrate Recovery Summit at Saddleback Church in 2004. Cheryl told me later that she didn't see these two being together. Mac looked too rough around the edges. We realized later that Mac was just a driven person, passionate about recovery and helping others find healing. And Mary was right by his side every step of the way, always smiling and looking for the best in others.

I kept my eye on this ministry leader as he soon became the Louisiana State Rep for Celebrate Recovery. We saw the Owens at some of the One Day seminars and Summits.

Each time we would pick up where we left off, sharing our lives with each other. Mac and I relate in our addictions, and now both of us are addicted to seeing changed lives. Cheryl and Mary love talking about kids and grandkids while giving people hope for restored relationships.

I saw how excited Mac was about Celebrate Recovery, how he couldn't keep quiet about it and talked to people about it wherever he went. I appointed him as the National CR Assimilation Coach, and today he serves as the National Director of the West. Mary was a natural at encouraging others. So Cheryl and I asked her to become the National CR Encourager Coach for women. They are a great team serving together.

Over the years they've become two of our dearest friends. We travel with Mac and Mary all over the world sharing about Celebrate Recovery at One Day seminars and the East and West Coast Summits.

You may have heard them share their testimony at a seminar or on a "Testimonies to Go" DVD, but you haven't heard the whole story! I don't think Travis Thrasher could have conjured up a fictional story any more dramatic than the profound truth of what God has done in Mac and Mary's lives.

Travis did an outstanding job on the novelization of *Home Run*. And now he has done it again, collaborating with the Owens to write their story in book form.

After you read Mac and Mary's story, you will see that people *can* change through Jesus Christ. And there is hope for you too. After you read their story, I pray you will take the next step to changing your life for the better. I look forward to hearing that your relationships are being restored, hurts are healing, and new healthy habits are being formed.

The things that are most important in life are our relationships. They are the only things we will take to heaven with us. Cheryl and I are thankful for our eternal relationship with Mac and Mary. We are truly Forever Family.

– John Baker
Founder of Celebrate Recovery

PREFACE

August 17, 1975

MY baby didn't even have a name.

I lay on the narrow and uncomfortable hospital bed feeling my insides leaking out. I realized I was no longer in labor, though the pain still tore through me. While I was unconscious, they had taken the baby and left me alone in this colorless, lifeless room. Alone to cry out in pain. Alone to contemplate what I had done. What *we* had done.

The baby I'd carried around for nine months, the baby nobody except Mac and my father knew about, was gone. Just like that. And I didn't even know if it was a boy or a girl.

I felt naked and abandoned. Yet more than that, I felt ashamed.

There was an emptiness inside of me I knew would never be filled. The memory of this room would be a reminder of what we had done, of the shameful consequence of our sin.

God help me, I prayed.

But I wondered if God was gone too. Maybe He wasn't going to come back either.

All I wanted was to know if my baby was breathing and alive and healthy. I wanted to see his little face and touch his little cheeks. I wanted to hear her little cry and see her little life.

The tears streaming down my face would never fill this hole inside of me.

This was my curse. And nobody else would ever—ever—know about it.

PART ONE

ALL OUR SORROWS, ALL OUR TEARS

1

FOOLED AROUND AND FELL IN LOVE

THE first thing I noticed was his hair. This big, bobbing mound of hair moving toward me down the school hallway. It was May 1974, and I was almost finished with my junior year at West Monroe High School in Louisiana. It was a big high school with a graduating class of four hundred students, but I knew I'd never seen this guy before. I would have remembered Mac Owen. Anybody who's ever met Mac remembers him.

Trouble had landed me in the hallway that school morning. I'd been talking in American history class and was sent outside to stand by the door. Little did I know that trouble would also be walking down that hallway wearing a blue plaid flannel shirt, baggy jeans, and suede shoes. Everything about this guy was cool. He walked past me and said hi, and I noticed he had the brightest eyes I'd ever seen. And just the sweetest smile. The sweetest, most mischievous smile.

Two things filled my mind instantly.

He's cute.

Where did he come from?

I kept thinking about this new student the rest of the day, wondering what his name was and where he'd come from. It wasn't long before I heard rumors. There had been a big drug bust at our school a few weeks earlier, and kids had discovered that the narc had been posing as a student at school. So when Mac showed up, a rumor started that he might be a narc too.

That rumor died quickly as people began getting to know him. "Mac can't be a narc. He's too cool."

Indeed, Mac wasn't the narc. In fact, he was one of those who should've been busted.

If anyone in my family should have written a memoir, it's my father. Alton Howard was born in 1925 on a small cotton farm in Rocky Branch, Louisiana. In the summertime he would pick cotton for three cents a pound so that his mama could buy his overalls and shoes for the next school year. Though he grew up in a poor house, his parents instilled rich values in their six children: to love each other, serve God, and work hard with integrity.

During World War II, Dad served his country as a navigator for B-26 airplanes. Several years later he married my mother, Jean Meador Howard. Of all the things my dad was to encounter in his life, the biggest challenge was seeing his young wife stricken with an illness that doctors knew very little about in the fifties and would later be categorized as schizophrenia. Dad took seriously the vows he'd made to Mama, and his unwavering love for her for fifty-seven years is part of his legacy to his three children.

Over the years, my father was involved in a variety of successful business endeavors, starting with Howard Bros. Jewelers, which he and his brother opened in 1946. A few years later they opened a discount store that eventually grew into the successful chain called Howard Bros. Discount Stores. The first Super Saver Whole Warehouse Club, which was later sold to Walmart and became part of the Sam's Club chain, was created by my father and my brother in 1986. His other businesses included an insurance company, restaurants, men's and women's clothing stores, oil and gas operations, and a music business.

As a gifted musician, Dad loved singing and writing hymns. Because of that love he founded Howard Publishing Company, where he was able to edit and produce several hymnals. Over three million copies have been sold and are still being used in congregations all over the world.

Despite all of Dad's successes, his greatest sense of achievement was the love he had for our Lord, our family, and God's church. He taught his three children the same values he had learned from his own parents: love and service and integrity and hard work. He spent his life and his money seeking to further God's Kingdom.

One example of this was the land my father donated to the church to create a Christian youth camp, Camp Ch-Yo-Ca, in 1967. When I was a little girl, he used to take me squirrel hunting on that property—one hundred acres of forest with southern yellow pines and majestic oaks and a lake perfect for canoeing and fishing. The camp continues to bless thousands of lives today, and I know it blessed ours. Because Camp Ch-Yo-Ca was where I fell in love with that bright-eyed cutie named Mac Owen.

There were a boys village and a girls village at Camp Ch-Yo-Ca, each with six cabins and a bathhouse. There was no air-conditioning anywhere, so needless to say, everybody was sweating all the time. The swimming pool between the two villages was the best place to cool off. Also between the two villages were a dining hall, kitchen, gym, and country store. Kids played on the softball field or by the volleyball nets, or got really good at Ping-Pong, or practiced crafts in the craft shed, or simply hung out by the swings.

Since this was a Christian camp with strict rules, girls had to wear long pants during the day and dresses at night for church services. Remember, we're talking Louisiana in the summer with hundred-degree weather. There was no "mixed swimming," either. Sometimes the boys would try to sneak over and peek through the fence at the girls swimming. They would get in huge trouble if they got caught, and even bigger trouble if they ever dared to sneak into the girls village.

Despite these strict rules, it was really a fun camp. Some of the best moments came late at night sitting by the campfire and listening to devotions and learning new camp songs. God worked on a lot of hearts at Camp Ch-Yo-Ca, and many kids came to faith in Christ and were baptized there before leaving.

Mac Owen attended White's Ferry Road Church of Christ just like I did, so it was no surprise that he ended up attending camp that June after he moved to West Monroe. Though we had barely spoken during his first month at our high school, I was glad to see that mushroom of hair in the camp dining hall or on the softball field. I always seemed to know exactly where Mac was that week, especially on nights when the stars filled the sky and curiosity filled my soul. I wanted to be close to him and find out what he was like. Just because we were attending a little Christian camp with two hundred kids didn't mean we'd been shut off from the rest of the world. It was the seventies, and lots of kids our age loved being as "cool" as they could be. Mac was part of the cool crowd, and I liked hanging out with them.

I'd been coming to this camp since I was in third grade. I had always wanted to please God, yet by the time I met Mac, I was curious about the world. Now here was this good-looking guy who I knew was cool and liked to make people laugh. How could I not want to hang around with him? I'd heard enough about God and knew what He thought about partying and having fun. But I was young and could get serious later. I wasn't going to hurt anybody.

On the last night of camp I watched Mac by the campfire. His face was lit up by the flames as he sat there, talking and making those around him laugh. When I caught him looking my way, I quickly averted my eyes. I could feel my heart racing as I watched the flames and thought about him. Despite all the talk over the past ten days about God and what He wanted out of my life, all I could think about was this cute guy I wanted to get to know…though I still didn't know exactly how I was going to end up sitting by his side.

It turned out I wasn't the only shy one. The following evening after the closing ceremony, at which we sang songs for our parents and accepted awards, one of Mac's friends came up to me looking as if he was holding the biggest secret in the world.

"Would you go out with Mac tonight if he asked you?" this boy said.

I smiled and nodded. "Yes, but he has to come ask me."

I might have been shy, but I wasn't going to make this easy for him.

Eventually Mac, hands in the pockets of his baggy jeans, blue jean shirt mirroring his bright-blue eyes, walked over to ask me out. We were both smiling, knowing he'd made sure I'd say yes first. I was all in, though I was nervous too, with a stomach full of butterflies. After he walked off to get his suitcase from his cabin, I looked at my girlfriends, and we all jumped up and down, holding hands and squealing.

Some moments are frozen in time.

It was June 1974, and the world seemed ready to explode into something wild and different and new. Some big scandal in Washington called Watergate was all everybody could talk about. America's time in Vietnam was over, even though fighting still went on over there. It was the last summer nobody paid any attention to movies and box office results; a year later, a movie about a shark would change all that.

It was the night after the end of camp, and I sat next to Mac as he drove my parents' brown Buick station wagon, full of couples who had gone to camp. The air outside was thick and made you stick to the car seat. Janice, my younger sister, was sitting next to a boy in the backseat. Station wagons back then had a third seat and were like minibuses, so we had a lot of kids in the car. The music was blaring and everybody was laughing and talking about camp memories. It felt so right to be sitting there next to this boy I barely knew.

I can't remember the exact song that was playing. Maybe it was a soft and tender ballad like The Eagles' "Desperado" that suddenly swept us up. Maybe it was rocking and pounding like Led Zeppelin's "When the Levee Breaks" that gave us a blast of courage and threw away our shyness. Maybe it was the funky "Long Train Runnin'" by the Doobie Brothers.

Whatever it was, the song on the radio didn't compare to the song in my heart. At a red light by the Louisana Power and Light Company, while the music played and the cars passed in front of us, Mac leaned over and kissed me.

It was tender and rocking and made my heart skip a beat. It was all that and more. Like the Grand Funk Railroad song, it was truly "Some Kind of Wonderful."

The next day I came down with scarlet fever.

A couple of weeks later, Mac called me on the phone. "Where have you been?" he asked.

"I thought you knew—I'm sick. I have some kind of rash or something."

It would have been fitting to joke with Mac that I'd picked up the scarlet fever from him. It would have also been fitting to tell him I felt like this was an omen, a premonition of things to come. Of course I would have been joking, and of course I didn't think any of those things. All I thought was *How long am I going to have this rash and not be able to see him?*

But the next thing I knew, someone was knocking at our front door. Mac had hitchhiked to my house, which was probably about twenty minutes from his. Today that doesn't seem like a great distance, but back then for two teenagers not connected by texting and the Internet, it felt pretty far.

I looked at the big-haired boy standing on my doorstep. "What are you doing here?" I asked.

All Mac did was smile. He wasn't going away anytime soon.

2

HYPNOTIZED

WE were escaping from the rest of the world.

Mary looked so tiny behind the wheel of her parents' station wagon. So tiny and so beautiful. It was November, and there were still red and orange leaves on the trees. The windows were down and her hair was blowing and I wouldn't have minded if she'd kept driving all the way to California. I wouldn't have stopped staring, either.

I remembered the first time I saw her at school, this pretty and shy girl standing outside her classroom for some reason. I had spotted her at church the Sunday before, which had made me think I might need to stay away from her. I had enough religion in my life. Yet I thought she might be cool because of the way she dressed. Bell-bottom jeans with decorative patches sewn all over them, and a blue-and-purple-and-fuchsia halter top. She even had on leather huaraches.

Now, months later, I knew Mary quite well. And liked her a lot too.

Since the summer we'd spent a lot of time with each other. I loved going over to Mary's house, but she didn't feel the same about coming to mine, as she was a bit intimidated by my father. She thought he was too gruff, which back then was probably true.

When we were young kids, my brother and I always got our haircuts on the military base. They cost a nickel, and the line was always "high on the sides and just enough on top to comb it." Whenever it was time to move, it wasn't as though my father paused and thought about letting us kids finish the school year. It felt more like "Okay, time to go. Get your stuff; get in the car; you have ten seconds to tell everybody you know good-bye." That's just the way it was. When the government told you to move, you moved.

By the time I was sixteen years old, living in West Monroe and crazy about Mary, I didn't have much of a relationship with my dad. So one way to show that was to grow out my hair and make everybody's life miserable. (I still love that 'fro and sometimes threaten that I'm going to grow it back out, but Mary wins out on this one; I have to live with her.)

Our parents raised us with good Christian values and we both—but especially Mary—knew it would hurt them so much if we got into trouble. But they didn't need to know what Mary and I did when we were together. I was old enough to know that some things were best left unspoken. In fact, that had already been demonstrated to me in our family in a very big way.

It's funny how in a lot of families you don't talk about the elephant in the room. I grew up in one of those families where you didn't share stuff. Stuff like the fact of my dad having been married before. I never knew about that until I was ten years old and someone referred to my older siblings as my half brother and half sister.

"They are not," I said.

"Yeah, they are."

"Nah," I said. "Why do you think that?"

"Have you ever seen your mom and dad's wedding pictures?"

Of course I had. They were front and center in our house. "Yeah."

"Who's in the picture? Your brother and sister!"

I couldn't believe it. I went and checked, and sure enough, there they were! Right away I asked Dad about it.

"How'd they get in the picture?" I asked.

"Don't worry about it."

When my dad said things like this, I understood. He was also saying, "Don't talk about it."

Yeah, those elephants stomping around in the room can be funny. They can also be pretty powerful when you set them free.

My father grew up in Old Hickory, Tennessee. Since his father died at an early age, Joe Owen had to become the man of the house of four siblings. He left to join the Army at a young age and soon got married. He was deployed to Germany, leaving his wife and their two young children behind.

By the time my father met my mother in Monterey, California, he was divorced and raising the two kids himself. Carla Ashley had grown up in West Texas. Her father, a school principal, died when she was young, and her mother, a schoolteacher, took the kids to California to be near family. My mother had recently graduated from Abilene Christian University; she and my father met while going to church in Monterey.

I was born there at Fort Ord Army base. We moved to Giessen, Germany, then to Fort Lewis, Washington, where we lived in Spanaway. We went back to Baumholder, Germany, then moved to Fort Benning in Columbus, Georgia. Then we moved back to California to San Lorenzo. We had one more army move, to Fort Lee in Petersburg, Virginia.

Now try to remember all *that* when you're asked where you grew up.

When I was nine years old, Dad was deployed to this place I'd never heard of before: Vietnam. Our family went to California to live with our grandmother while he served his time. I remember Dad would tape his voice onto a reel-to-reel and mail it to us. We would sit in my grandmother's house, circling the stereo, and listen to Dad's voice speaking to us. At this time my two older siblings were already out of the house, so it was just me and my two younger brothers, David and Joe. My little sister, Becky, was born later that year, right before he got back from Vietnam.

At night we would all sit around the television listening to Walter Cronkite talk about what was happening in the war. In his dark suit and tie and slicked-back hair, the newscaster would share the daily happenings in a world that seemed so remote and far away. I tried to imagine my father in the places they showed, but I didn't really want to think about it. I didn't want to think of him being hurt or, even worse, dying and leaving all of us behind. Listening to those tapes of him speaking would remind us he was safe. At least for the moment.

It would have been easy for my father to start drinking and using drugs while in the service, but Dad did the opposite. He was a Christian and he wanted that to stand for something. He had always been one to share the gospel with other people, and when his assignment at Fort Lee was over and he retired from the military, he decided to go to seminary to become a full-time evangelist. That's what brought us to what I believed was the armpit of the world, West Monroe...and what brought me to Mary.

With Dad's stand on drinking and drug use, and a mother who probably never touched a drop of alcohol in her life, things like smoking cigarettes and drinking were strictly forbidden in our house. It's pretty ironic who first introduced me to dope.

I was twelve years old and living in Virginia. I had discovered that if you smoke cigarettes, there was an immediate acceptance with a whole group of people that you didn't have to prove anything to. As a young kid who moved around a lot, smoking cigarettes was all about acceptance, pure and simple.

One summer my father cooked for a few weeks at Camp Idlewild, a church camp. We happened to be between sessions, with only the staff and their family members around. One of the counselors—let's call him Tom—knew I smoked cigarettes, so one night he asked if I wanted to try something new, something that would make me feel really good. I said, "Sure."

By the time I entered Mary's life, the philosophy of "Sure" had followed me into every shadowy corner I could find. For instance, on the third day of attending West Monroe High School, some guys suspected I was a narc, so they tested me.

"If you're one of us, then why don't you try some of these mushrooms?"

"Mushrooms?" I said. "What do you do with mushrooms? The only thing we do with them is put them on pizza."

"Not these mushrooms," they said.

You can guess what I said.

"Sure!"

So they gave them to me before school that morning, and by about second period I was thinking, *These guys sure know how to party.*

The party wouldn't be over for a very long time.

So on that clear and calm November Friday, the thought of spending the afternoon inside a classroom listening to a teacher ramble on made my head hurt. I'd skipped school before and knew that Mary's parents were gone. Her mother was in the hospital and her father was on a business trip. I just wanted to go hang out with her on this beautiful fall day. Yet I was a bit surprised when Mary agreed.

It wasn't like I had one thing and one thing only on my mind. I mean, I always had *that* on my mind. I'd even resorted occasionally to the old familiar line of "If you loved me…" But on this day I really and truly wanted to hang out with her, just have some fun and nothing more. If something more happened, then that'd be cool.

We listened to Janis Joplin's *In Concert* album as we sat on Mary's bed in her room. I couldn't believe we were there, all by ourselves, with no worries of someone knocking on the door or checking in on us. Her bedroom didn't just feel cozy and cute. It felt intimate. I knew I was somewhere I probably shouldn't be, but both of us wanted to be there, listening to music and forgetting the rest of the world and thinking we were older than we were.

We'd been inseparable ever since we met, and we'd already been getting pretty physical on our dates, but on this day, it just happened. It happened quickly, and all I could think was *What in the world is happening?* all while Janis serenaded the two of us. Afterward, both Mary and I seemed to be shocked and amazed, asking if we'd really just done that. Neither of us had ever had sex before, and it wasn't something we'd really spoken to many people about. Especially not our parents. One part of me was like *Wow, that was pretty cool* and another part was like *Wait a minute—what did we just do?*

Of course, when I saw Mary the next day, the hesitant part of me had gone away and the excited part was reminding her how cool it had been. Mary wasn't just hesitant; she seemed a bit scared with what we'd done. She said it couldn't happen again; we had to wait.

I didn't want to wait. What were we waiting for?

3

CHILD OF MINE

I stared at the familiar Bible verses, searching for an answer, even though I already knew what I needed to do. I was locked in the bathroom before school started. I had already thrown up, as I did almost every morning. I brushed my teeth to get rid of the bitter taste while I glanced at the dozens of three-by-five index cards taped on the tile starting halfway up the wall. These were my mother's gift to our family, and normally they brought me comfort. Now they only seemed to bring shame and confusion.

You know how a lot of people read magazines in the bathroom? In the Howard household on Johnathan Street, we read passages of Scripture. The walls were covered with index cards written in my mother's handwriting. They weren't just in our personal bathrooms; verses were taped up in the powder room that guests used too. She wrote the verses from the King James Version using block letters.

I would read them over and over without even thinking about what the verses meant.

Mom wrote out verses for herself, too, on the white cardstock that panty hose were wrapped around in their packaging. The five-by-seven size. She would leave them on her dresser, on her nightstand, in her bathroom, and on the counter by the telephone in the kitchen. Her Bible was stuffed with her cardstock verses as well.

When we went to bed at night, she quoted Scripture to us, like Isaiah 41:10: "Fear thou not; for I am with thee: be not dismayed; for I am thy God: I will strengthen thee; yea, I will help thee; yea, I will uphold thee with the right hand of my righteousness." In the morning she would wake us up with Philippians 4:4: "Rejoice in the Lord always: and again I say, Rejoice." I once believed she did this for all of us, but as I grew older and learned more about her illness, I realized Mom quoted Scripture for her own self and soul.

On this particular morning, a mural of verses faced me as usual. For the past couple of months, I had been waking up feeling nauseated. Sometimes I would throw up in the school bathroom before classes. But I didn't know anything about morning sickness, and there was no such thing as Google to take my questions to. I thought I was just sick from worrying that I might be pregnant.

I sought the wall for encouragement. Romans 8:28 told me that all things worked together for good to those who loved God. Ephesians 6:11 told me to put on the full armor of God that I would be able to stand against the wiles of the devil. Proverbs 3:5 told me to trust in the Lord with all my heart and not to lean on my own understanding. Ephesians 6:1 told me to obey my parents in the Lord because this was right.

So many verses with so much advice, yet none of them seemed to give me any answers. They just made me feel more guilt and worry.

I knew I needed to talk to a doctor, but I tried to bury that reality a little longer. I was fine. I was just worried. Nobody got pregnant from their first time. It was a stupid thought. I knew a lot of girls who had sex all the time and didn't get pregnant. I was positive I'd get my period any day...even though I hadn't gotten it for two months.

I shut off the light and left the room of God's reminders behind in darkness. It would take a little while longer before they would finally catch up to me.

It was amazing how I could have kept this secret from everyone except Mac. Amazing and crazy. I hadn't even told my best friend that I thought I might be pregnant. Finally I went to the doctor to see if something was wrong with me. He stared at me in disbelief. I could see the contempt in his narrow eyes.

"You are four months pregnant," he said, shaking his head. "How could you not know?"

His words mocked me, making me feel stupid and naive. I wasn't sure what to say. Every word that came to mind seemed insignificant and hollow, just like I felt.

"I'm calling your parents right now. They need to know."

I begged and pleaded with him not to tell them. I would do it myself, I told him; I *needed* to tell them myself. I wasn't sure how or when, but I couldn't let this doctor tell them.

My legs felt weak and wobbly as I left his office wiping the tears off my face. I needed to figure out a plan. I would talk to Mac and come up with something. It was March of my senior year. I only had a couple months left of school.

How can I keep this secret from everyone else?

I felt ashamed and stupid.

All I wanted was for this—for *all* of this—to just go away.

As I got back into my car, I shivered when I thought of what I might tell my parents. Then I realized I could only tell my father. My mother couldn't know. Not now. Not in her condition.

The thought of her knowing I was pregnant scared me even more than the realization that I was carrying a child.

The first time my father knew something was wrong with my mother was when my older brother, Johnny, was just a little bitty baby. One day my father woke up and heard him crying. When he got up, he saw my mother sitting on the floor just holding little Johnny, a haunting, blank stare on her face.

"Jean, what's the matter?" he asked. "You going to feed the baby?"

Mom wouldn't move. Johnny was just lying in her arms, fussing and crying. This went on for two days.

My parents were young and hadn't been married long. They had been so full of love and life. My father had no idea what to do. He eventually called a doctor and explained what was happening.

"I don't know what's wrong with my wife. She won't feed the baby; she won't eat; she won't get up and get dressed; she won't talk. She's just sitting on the floor like a zombie or something."

The doctor said, "Bring her to the hospital."

Back in those days, when somebody acted like this, they just counted them crazy and put them in a state hospital. You never saw them again. Well, my father wasn't about to go for that. He told the doctors, "No, we're going to figure out what's wrong with her."

In a short time doctors explained that she had had a nervous breakdown, and my mother started going in and out of hospitals. My parents' battle with this unknown illness had begun. My mother went through several years of getting treated by hospitals and using all kinds of drugs. Eventually a doctor told my father a theory.

"We've heard that sometimes patients get better when they're pregnant."

So my father said, "Let's try to have another baby."

Mom got pregnant with me, and she did get better. While she was pregnant, she seemed to be her old self. Yet after she had me, she went spiraling back down again. She wouldn't eat or drink, but would just stand in the corner in the kitchen. She was never violent, except for when my father would have to take her to the hospital. Then she would kick and scream and say, "No, please don't take me!"

She knew that going to the hospital meant shock treatments and other awful things meant to help her.

The term *paranoid schizophrenic* didn't mean anything to my father or our family. All he knew was that the woman he'd committed his life to was suddenly sick with some kind of terrible illness.

Several weeks after seeing the doctor, I almost told my father the truth. Almost.

It was April and a beautiful spring day, and my father asked me to go fishing. We went to Camp Ch-Yo-Ca, the same summer camp where I first met Mac. It seemed like an ideal place to tell him the news.

I was almost five months pregnant, yet I had developed an art to hiding my growing belly. On this day I wore a big bright-orange shirt with hippos all over it that I had made myself. My bulge was perfectly camouflaged. We paddled out onto the lake in an aluminum canoe with our fishing poles. The water was calm and the camp was completely quiet. The blue sky above us stretched for miles in every direction. We made small talk, with my father asking me about school and college.

For a moment as we sat there in that small boat, I sensed he was waiting for me to say something, to tell the truth.

Does he know?

I couldn't tell but wanted to believe he didn't, the same way I had wanted to believe that I wasn't pregnant for those four months before visiting a doctor.

What's he going to say if I tell him?

It seemed as though everything around us went silent. I didn't speak, and the moment passed.

I knew, however, that whatever happened, I had to tell my father. So shortly after that time in the canoe, I devised a plan. I told my best friend, Denise, that I was pregnant and had her ask her parents if I could move in with them during the summer. They were moving to Robeline, Louisiana, which was far enough away to keep my pregnancy a secret from everybody I knew. They said yes immediately, so over the next few days I gathered my courage to approach my father and tell him what I was going to do.

Daddy always came home from work for lunch, after which he usually took a thirty-minute nap on the couch in the family room. This was a huge sectional couch at least twenty feet long that went halfway around our den. I had snuggled with my father many times on this couch while he read Bible verses and spoke to me about God's love.

A round marble-top coffee table sat in front of the couch. On this day, I sat down on the rug between the coffee table and the couch to get eye to eye with my father and nudge him awake.

"We need to talk," I said in a quiet voice.

My father listened as I told him the truth: I was five months pregnant and Mac Owen was the father and I planned on living with my best friend's family that summer and we intended to give the baby up for adoption and we weren't going to tell anybody else including Mom and nobody would know the truth since I was due in August.

I stared at my father, expecting anger and judgment. I could imagine the sort of things it would have been easy for him to say. He was an elder in our church, and nobody in our congregation had ever gotten pregnant outside of marriage. Not only that, but he was a respected businessman who ran a Christian publishing business. Combined with my mother's illness, he already had a lot to deal with. He would have every right to point his finger and lash out at me for making such a huge mistake.

Yet those soft eyes only showed love spilling out of them. Tears streamed down his cheeks as he hugged me. "I knew you were pregnant because I could see your belly," he said, confirming what I had suspected. "I kept thinking maybe if I didn't say the words out loud, it wouldn't be true." He embraced me for a moment; then he looked me in the eyes and said the words I not only wanted but needed to hear: "Mary, I will love you always. And I'll support whatever decision you make."

I was seventeen and a senior in high school, and I thought I had a lot of things figured out. Yet I couldn't understand my father's response. I couldn't believe he supported my decision and still loved me despite what I had done.

"This has never happened to anybody else we know," I managed to say through my choking tears. "You'll be kicked out of the eldership, and it will be my fault. Mac is too young and irresponsible to marry. And what will this do to Mother? I have no choice but to move away… I want my baby to have a good life…Surely there is a married couple who can't have children who would give him the life he deserves."

My patient and loving father nodded and said he would talk to a lawyer about it.

So Mac and I had a plan. Soon we could put this behind us and move on with our lives.

God, of course, had another plan. And it was far better than Mac or I or my father or anybody else could imagine.

4

TAKE IT EASY

June 8, 1975

Dear Mary:

Camp wasn't the same this year without you. A lot of people asked about you. I told them you're in California on a senior trip having lots of fun. Some even asked if we were still dating and I told them yeah. If they only knew.

I made a walking stick out of a dogwood tree during Bible class one day. It reminds me of you 'cause I carved your name in it.

Good news: it looks like I'm gonna be working for the maintenance crew this summer around camp. Should be fun. Some of the guys are real cool.

Saw your dad at camp but didn't talk to him. It was a little scary seeing him, so I steered clear.

By the way—wanted to let you know what happened at church the other day. Jack, the elder I've never gotten along with, came up to me and said, "I know what you have done!" And believe me, even though he is not in active duty, he is still every bit a Marine.

He put his finger right in my face said he knew I'd gotten you pregnant. I told him I didn't know what he was talking about.

I miss you, Mary. I wish I could see you. Could you take a picture to send me? Just one? Nobody will see it. I just want to see what you look like. I know you look beautiful. I wish we could be together.

My birthday's coming up, and I'm thinking about maybe coming to see you. I've got something in mind. Gotta see if it'll work out.

I love you and can't wait until I see you again.

Mac

June 12, 1975

Dear sweet, sweet Mac:

Denise, Jeff, and Mrs. J just went shopping, so I thought I would write you, even though I'll be calling you in an hour. I got your letter today. It was so beautiful as usual, and the pictures just brightened my day. Thank you.

I am sending you this picture to show you how little my niece, Korie, was just last summer. Isn't she precious? Don't lose it, because it is one of the pictures from my album. I don't have very many, but when I get home, we are going to take pictures all the time.

Jaws sounds like a good movie. I've seen the previews on TV, but I doubt it will ever make it to Robeline.

Today Denise and I watched some cowboys round up the cows to move them to another pasture. It was really interesting because I've never seen it done in real life.

The candy you sent me really is delicious but it's nearly gone. Every time I walk into the bedroom, either Jeff or Denise is getting a handful. I guess they really like it too. Ha-ha.

I talked to Mother on the phone last night. She was so excited and so was I. She told me I better hurry up and come home because she misses me so much. She really sounded good on the phone.

Oh, Mac, I just can't wait to get home. I love you so immensely that I feel like I'm going to burst. It is just so hard to contain myself. To not be able to show my love to you is driving me crazy. Oh happy day, when I get home.

You know I still feel the same way about us "holding off" until we are married. One thing always leads to another. I know we can do it because we love each other so much. We will just have to help one another.

Well, I need to get some clothes out of the dryer and then I will call you. Thank you for making me so happy. You know if there hadn't have been the preaching school in West Monroe, we might not have ever met?

All my love forever,

Mary

Mac—I opened this letter back up to tell you something. I talked to Denise and she doesn't think it's a good idea at all to send a picture. Please try to understand. I trust you completely, you know that. It's just that small chance of its being found. I just can't take that chance. I wouldn't even keep one in my own room at home. Please forgive me, darling. I feel bad about not doing it, but please understand. I know you will! I'll be home soon. I love you so very much. It was so wonderful to talk to you today.

You have all my love for eternity.

Your big butterball,

Mary

P.S. I want to see one of those beautiful smiles now. Sometimes I feel as though you are right beside me. I don't ever want you to let me go.

5

BEAUTIFUL CHILD

"GOD, please take care of this little baby."

I prayed these words every day as my tiny child grew.

Sometimes tears would fall. They felt as commonplace as my guilt and my loneliness. I knew God could see me and heard my prayers, but I still didn't know if He would answer them. My hand on my belly would feel the little kicks and punches, and all I wanted was for this little soul inside of me to have a good home and a good childhood.

"Bless this little life," I prayed.

I carried the promise of life around with me in a sanctuary of shame. Some days I didn't know what to do with myself. I wanted to go back home to my life and my family and my Mac. I missed them dearly. I wanted them to be walking by me during this journey. But I was alone.

I could imagine my baby in my arms, his soft skin against mine, her sweet little laugh lighting up the morning sky.

I had names picked out for either, names I'd have to go back to Monroe carrying inside me. Names that would never be used, tucked alongside memories that would never be made.

I knew everything in my life would change if I brought back our child and began raising him, yet I knew I could do it. We could do it. I would start thinking this way and wonder, *Can I? Should I?* Then reality would smack me across the face.

I imagined my church standing me up in the front on a Sunday morning in order to tar and feather shame all over me. I thought of my father and his place in the church and community. Then I thought of my mother, my poor sweet momma, and what she might do to herself.

Once I called up our lawyer about the possibility of keeping our child. Evidently the lawyer talked to my doctor, because the next time I went for a checkup, the doctor looked me in the eye and said: "You will put your mother in a mental institution *forever* if she *ever* finds out about this."

From that point on, I knew I couldn't let myself even consider it. I ached thinking about it, about the life inside of me and the mistake I had made and how much it might hurt and impact my family. I forced myself not to dwell on these things, yet they filled my heart and soul like water rushing through a broken levee.

My tears would wake up with me and follow me around like toddlers throughout the day. I would fall asleep in an empty bed even though there were two lives sleeping inside it. I would see my baby's round cheeks in my dreams.

I walked around feeling half-empty even while my belly felt so tight and full.

I told myself I had no choice

Yes you do, a voice would whisper back in the still of the day.

This wasn't what I wanted or Mac wanted, but what we needed to do.

Come to me, all you who are weary and burdened, and I will give you rest.

But I knew people would be mean and judge me and my baby if we came home.

Trust in the LORD with all thine heart; and lean not unto thine own understanding.

I had escaped my parents' house in Monroe and had gone undetected by my mother, yet I could still hear her influence through the verses that floated around in my head. I buried those too. I didn't want to hear from God, not during this time. I had let Him down, and I knew I had to go about this on my own.

Despite all that, I continued to pray. *Lord, watch over this precious little one inside of me.*

I felt like Moses' mother when she could no longer keep him and had to let him go by putting him in a basket in the bulrushes. I had no idea who would get my baby, but I prayed my child would be strong and mighty and taken care of. And I prayed I could see him just once before letting him go.

6

AIN'T SEEN NOTHING YET

THE music was loud, and we were rolling down the highway trying to forget about all those blues that wanted to get us down. The four of us in the car laughed a lot and smoked a lot. Well, three of us smoked while the mother-to-be next to me refrained. Every now and then I'd forget about everything and find myself laughing almost uncontrollably, being goofy, just loving being around Mary again.

It was the calm before the storm. Or maybe it was a storm before the calm, as the concert we were headed for was anything but calm—but it sure was soothing seeing Mary. And man, was I still crazy about her.

If you saw her from behind, you'd have no idea this petite and pretty girl was seven months pregnant. She'd done a great job of hiding her growing belly during the school year, but now there was no hiding it. Part of me didn't want her to. I wanted to tell the world. The problem was the world—especially our little corner of the world—didn't want to hear it.

I knew I wanted to spend the rest of my life with this girl. I just wasn't ready to settle down yet. I wasn't ready to get a job and get married and start a family. I mean, I was about to turn seventeen years old. I still had my senior year of high school left. We had our whole lives ahead of us. We just had to figure out what to do about the life growing in Mary's belly.

Mary's best friend, Denise, had moved with her family to the small farm town of Robeline, Louisiana, after graduation. It was the perfect place for Mary to hide out. To celebrate my birthday, I'd gotten tickets for the Bachman-Turner Overdrive show at Hirsch Memorial Coliseum in Shreveport. It felt just like old times, and it was fun to forget about everything, including the baby we planned on giving up. Yet both of us still had doubts.

"You sure you want to go through with this?" I asked her at one point during the day.

"You still have a year left of school," Mary reminded me. "We don't have money for a child. You're not ready to be a father. And I just can't do this to my mom and dad."

Even though I had a really good buzz going from smoking pot, I knew she was right. I wasn't ready to be a father. Later on, I was sure, when I became an official dad, I'd settle down and stop partying so much, but I wanted to make that decision when I was ready. Not now. I wasn't even ready for my senior year of high school.

The one thing I did know was this: I was ready to be with Mary. We just had this connection. She got me, and I didn't know if another person had ever gotten me my entire life. I felt like I could be myself around her, and that she was a good person inside and out. She was fun and could put up with me having more fun than she did. She loved my jokes, and she even loved the massive mound of hair on my head.

Yeah, I wasn't gonna let Mary go anytime soon. The only question was whether she'd get tired of me and figure out something else to do with her life.

You could feel the music deep in your gut. That was the reason to go to concerts, to celebrate with others this feeling deep down inside, this delirious joy that covered up the emptiness. Rock and roll filled those empty spaces, especially in a sold-out concert hall.

Bachman-Turner Overdrive was a high-energy, feel-good band. Everybody knew and sang the lyrics of their songs. They were really mainstream, the perfect sort of group to go see with Mary. She needed a little high-energy and a lot of feel-good vibes coming her way.

But to be honest, I liked the opening act better. Johnny Winter was a blues guitarist who could rock the house. The raucous "Bony Moronie" was one of my favorite songs, along with "Johnny B. Goode." The rocker sounded like some kind of wild wizard that night. Everybody moved and swayed to his guitar, and by then I was really flying high, so the music warmed my head and my heart. So did the girl rocking by my side.

By the time BTO jammed, Mary yelled in my ear to tell me she could feel the baby bouncing around in her belly. I put my hands on her belly and kept feeling the fist pumps coming my way. The concert was fun and crazy, and I was glad we were introducing this child to some good rocking music.

The reality was this: I didn't want to hurt anybody. I never wanted to cause anybody pain, especially this girl I was deeply in love with. I just wanted to have fun. *We* just wanted to have fun. People were so uptight with their rules and their religions. I just wanted to laugh and hang out and listen to music. That's what life was all about, right?

That was all that mattered. At least back then.

"I'll be fine," Mary told me right before I said good-bye to her later that night.

She said it in a way that made me believe her. She was strong and she'd get through this.

I gave her a farewell kiss, hoping her words would prove true. Man, was I young and stupid. I wish I could go back and slap some sense into that kid. To tell him he had no idea what Mary was about to go through and to explain that it wasn't going to be as simple as giving a record away to a buddy. No amount of drugs or music would drown out the reality of the choice we were making.

But you're only young once, and some decisions are irreversible.

Some end up haunting you for many years to come.

7

YOU'VE GOT A FRIEND

"HELP me!"

The echoes of my screams bounced around the bare walls of the hospital room. I had just awoken from being put under with a gas mask, and I thought I was still having the baby. The last thing I remembered was the doctor cutting me as they strapped the mask over my face. All I could think was *They're killing me. I'm dying. This is the end of my life.*

When I woke up, I felt like someone was sticking a blowtorch to my bottom. It burned like it was on fire. The pain was excruciating, and I began to howl.

A nurse came into the room and tried to silence me. "You're being too loud. You've had the baby; now you need to hush up and be quiet."

I was sobbing in my agony, and the revolving doctors and nurses coming into the room wouldn't tell me anything.

"Well, what did I have?" I asked them. "Did I have a boy or a girl?"

They refused to tell me, simply taking my vitals and showing no emotion on their faces. The only looks I received were judging, critical looks, the kind that said *How could you do something like this?* The kind that secretly whispered under their breath *Sinner* and *Shame on you* and *Such a sad, sad scene.*

The hospital staff treated me like a ghost, which made me start thinking the worse. Something had happened to the baby. *My baby's dead.*

"Please tell me something," I begged.

Yet they said nothing.

"Is it a boy or a girl? Is it alive or dead?"

No answers came. The most miraculous thing in my life had just occurred, yet I was isolated and angry and completely alone.

I'm being punished for my sins, I thought. For what we'd done and for the lie we were planning to maintain.

I thought I had all this figured out. This agony wasn't part of the plan. I was in a prison of my own making, and there was no escape in sight.

The plan had been to stay in Robeline until giving birth later in the summer. My father sent money to Denise's family to pay for my room and board. He paid my doctor bills.

He also paid a lawyer, who was a personal friend of the family, to find a couple to take the baby. Mac and I wanted our baby to be with a good Christian family who shared our faith—or at least shared my faith, since at that time

Mac wasn't a professing believer. Our one stipulation was that the family needed to live out of our town. I told my father, "If our child is here in town, I'll want him. I can't do this thing of seeing him and leaving."

So everything was kept confidential between my father and the lawyer; he would never tell us who the family was, what town they lived in, or any other details. Making matters even worse—or better, depending on how you looked at it—there were more laws back then regarding private adoptions. The adopting family had a lot of rights.

I knew I loved Mac, but I also knew we weren't ready to be married. I didn't know if we'd ever marry, not then. We were so young, and we were partiers. How would we make it? And if things didn't work out, divorce wasn't an option. Not back in those days.

So I kept telling myself, *The child will be better off.*

But suddenly, resting silently in the hospital, still feeling torn up inside and out, I wondered if the child *would* be better off. Or if the child was even alive.

My eyes were surely bloodshot after having cried all the tears they could. I felt weak and empty and completely worn out. I barely noticed the nurse walk in until he greeted me in a deep voice and asked how I was doing. When I looked up, I saw a face I hadn't seen before. For a second I thought I was dreaming, because surely this guy wasn't one of my nurses.

Before me stood the biggest black man I'd ever seen. He was handsome, with a bright smile, and I swear he looked almost shiny. Perhaps it was the light in the room and his outfit of all white, but he looked like he was almost glowing.

You have to remember something—this was Robeline, Louisiana, in the seventies. A highly segregated town, Robeline was a place where the Ku Klux Klan still burned crosses in fields. Discrimination was rampant, and as a culture we had a long way to go.

But standing before me was this massive black man dressed like a nurse. I blinked several times to make sure I wasn't dreaming, but the man still stood there.

"Why are you crying?" he asked as if he had no idea what had just happened.

"It's my baby. I just want to know—please, will you tell me if it's okay? Would you tell me if I had a boy or a girl?"

None of the other nurses had ever looked at me for longer than a second. Yet this man looked me square in the eyes in a calm and gentle way, then nodded and smiled at me.

"I'll find out," he said in a deep southern drawl. "You can't tell anybody, but I'll find out."

He left and then a few moments later walked back into my room. I stopped breathing for a moment, expecting to hear the worst.

"You have a beautiful baby boy. He's perfect in every way. He's got all his fingers and toes and he's absolutely beautiful."

The words felt like aloe poured over my burnt soul.

I started to weep.

I saw his big smile again as he said, "Don't tell anybody I told you, okay?"

"Thank you," I said weakly.

My boy was healthy and alive and absolutely beautiful.

The nurse walked out of my room and I never saw him again. He never came back around to check on me or even to say hi. Not once. I didn't see him passing by my room or out in the hallway or behind a desk.

God could have done the same thing to me that I was doing to my baby boy. He could have abandoned me. Instead, He gave me the only answer I wanted to know at that time. He allowed an angel to come in and tell me our baby was fine and beautiful and blessed.

My tears stopped, and in their place came thankfulness.

Despite everything I'd done, God wasn't giving up on me.

Around noontime, as I lay in my room all alone, I decided it was time to call my dad and tell him the news. As I dialed our home phone number, my hands shook. When he answered the phone, I said, "Daddy, it's Mary."

In the background was singing. For a moment I listened and realized I was hearing my whole family singing "Happy Birthday" to my sister. I started to weep.

My baby had been born on August 17, my sister's sixteenth birthday.

It also happened to be a Sunday, so our whole family was at our house having Sunday lunch. I could imagine the stories and the laughter and the conversation over a dining room table full of food. I could picture their faces, each one of them. I missed them all so dearly.

I wiped the tears away and cleared my throat as I tried to talk over their voices. Soon the singing stopped and my father knew it was me on the phone.

Be strong, Mary. Be tough.

There were so many things I wanted to say, yet I couldn't, not right then. So I kept it quick.

"Dad, I know you can't talk now because the whole family is in the room celebrating Janice's birthday. But I just wanted to tell you I had a little boy and he's healthy and everything is good. I'm doing fine. So I'll talk to you later."

That was all I said. He said good-bye and nothing else.

I can't imagine the burden he felt as he went back to the table with everybody in the family except me sitting there. I know he was worried and wished I were with them. I'm sure he wanted to tell them. What he didn't know at the time was that my brother and sister-in-law both knew, yet they were keeping this a secret too.

Johnny had heard some of the rumors and knew the lie that I'd told everybody: that I was going to California with my best friend, Denise. So he'd called Denise's mother in Robeline in order to try to connect the dots of what was really happening.

I happened to answer the phone that day. When he heard my voice, he hung up because it freaked him out so much. He called again, and soon both of us were crying on the phone. Chrys and Johnny eventually came down to see me.

They even offered to take care of the baby for me, an offer I knew I couldn't allow.

"No—there's no way," I told them. "I really appreciate that, but if my baby comes home, I'm going to take care of it. That's not the problem."

I told them what the doctor said would happen to our mother if she learned I was pregnant—that she'd be in a mental institution the rest of her life. I couldn't do that to my mother or to our family.

So Johnny and Chrys were also keeping our secret.

There was so much silence and so many secrets inside our family. Even though I believed they were necessary to keep our family intact, they felt like unbelievable burdens…too big and heavy to go away.

The next day Denise and I sneaked down to the nursery to see what we could find. First we had asked a nurse whether we could simply see my baby boy, but she told us she'd need to check with my lawyer. When she came back, the stern look on her face hadn't gone away.

"No, you can't see the baby."

But I was determined to try for even a glance at him. So later that day I gathered up the energy to climb out of bed. I hobbled down the hallways with Denise by my side, both of us trying to keep our giggling as quiet as possible.

When we arrived at the window to the nursery, I stood there holding my breath. There was only one baby there, in the very back of the room, as if he was deliberately being kept away from the window. His front faced the wall, so all I could see was the back of his little head. I saw the hair sticking out and was reminded of the day I first saw that guy with the big mound of hair walking down the hallway at school.

"That must be him," I told Denise. "I bet you anything that's him."

He looked so tiny in his bassinet. He had been with me for nine months. Now he looked so far away.

The next day my lawyer came to the hospital with the papers that would make everything official.

"Can I see him?" I asked. "I just want to hold him one time."

He shook his head. "No, no, you can't. If you're going to give him up for adoption, you don't need to see him. You just need to forget about him."

He didn't say this in a mean tone. He was just speaking the truth. He was saying, "This is how you need to do it if you're going to give him up" because he knew that if I held my baby in my arms, I might not give him up. And everything would have totally changed.

So I signed the papers and let our child go. As quick and simple as that. With one small signature.

The still of night came to my room at the hospital. I felt tired and depleted. Yet most of all, I felt alone. Once again

I imagined what our son's face looked like, how soft his skin felt, what his hoarse cry might sound like.

My hands and my arms were empty, just like my heart.

I believed it was the best decision we could make. I knew these feelings would go away in time. Eventually I would stop thinking of the child I would never be able to picture, the name I would never know.

Eventually I would give him up fully and completely.

Well…that's what I told myself anyway. Even if I knew deep down it wasn't true.

8

THE SONG REMAINS THE SAME

LOOK—it wasn't all sadness and tragedy back then. The party continued, and Mary and I joined in the fun. Remember, I was seventeen and a senior in high school who couldn't find my locker the entire year. She was eighteen, working at Howard Bros. Warehouse. We didn't stop and think back on what happened or let it rule our lives. We kept on living. We kept on partying.

And hey—we enjoyed ourselves. When the only person you have to please is yourself and you have no responsibilities, why shouldn't you enjoy yourself? Who was watching?

Back then, I doubted God was that concerned with what a bunch of teenagers were doing in West Monroe, Louisiana. Was there even a God above? Sometimes I'd wonder, especially when I was high on pot or mushrooms.

We weren't hurting anybody. Even if, at times, we sure had the potential of hurting ourselves.

There were many outdoor activities to keep us busy. Like skiing, for instance.

Now I know what you're thinking. Skiing in Louisiana? Don't ever let anybody tell you that folks from our home state aren't creative.

(Disclaimer: the following incident is not in any way endorsed by Mary and Mac Owen but is included here to demonstrate the stupidity that partying can and will cause the partygoer.)

One of our friends named Sonny owned an MG (one of those two-seater British sports cars). A guy would tie a rope to the back bumper of the car and then, after enough alcohol, somebody would be brave (meaning stupid) enough to grab the rope and yell to Sonny, "Hit it!" Sonny would then pull the person down the dirt road.

Needless to say, there were many more failed attempts than successful ones. Most of us ended up with a smile full of dirt as we tasted the sweet dust of the country road. Of course, as the crowd cheered us on, there was always someone else who would pick the rope up and try again. At these parties on the weekends, there might be anywhere from thirty to a hundred people attending.

Along with partying all the time, we often went camping. We would have a convoy of vehicles following each other up into the Arkansas mountains, sometimes arriving well past midnight. It would be too late to set up tents, so the first night we'd sleep in our sleeping bags on the ground or in our vehicles. Once after an unexpected cold front moved in, we woke up to snow sprinkled in our hair. Even though it was bitter cold, I still loved it. A cup of coffee in hand, the sizzle of bacon cooking on a propane stove, the view of majestic bluffs. Soon we'd have camp all set up.

Mary and our friends and I canoed down many rivers together in Arkansas, Georgia, Tennessee, South Carolina, and West Virginia. They had names like Piney, Nantahala, Ocoee, Chattahoochee, and Gauley. We even went out on the Chattooga, where the movie *Deliverance* was filmed. (And no, I didn't hear any banjos in the background.) Sometimes we took all of our gear with us in the canoes, and we wouldn't see civilization for two or three days. But most of the time, after setting up camp, we would canoe down a river for the day and catch a shuttle back to camp by sundown. After a hearty meal cooked over a fire, we would sit around the campfire laughing and recounting all the adventures we'd had that day.

Of course, like the clouds in the sky above, the drugs were always there. I could say it was a part of the culture and the times, but it didn't matter what period of life I was living in. Simply put, I enjoyed getting high. It became as ordinary as waking up and having a morning cup of coffee. It made everything a lot smoother—from coasting down those winding rivers to late-night conversations.

Another fun memory from back in those days is of our visits to the zoo after midnight.

(Disclaimer: These incidents are in no way endorsed by Mary and Mac Owen but are included here to demonstrate how thankful they are there wasn't such a thing as YouTube back in those days. No animals were killed or permanently damaged in the following scenes.)

One of our friends was a night watchman at the zoo in Monroe, so at midnight we would load up a feed wagon with cases of beer and pull it around the zoo to check out the animals. Rosie the orangutan mimicked everything we did, including smoking cigarettes and joints. She sat in a circle with us, taking a hit off the joint or cigarette and then passing it to the next person. Then, because we were drinking beer, she would hold her hand out for a can of beer too. It was like she was getting a brief escape from the cage she was living in.

Then there was the hippo who appeared to be waiting on us to come in. As soon as we walked in the door, she would come to the front of the bars, open her huge mouth, and wait for us to pour a beer in. After two or three beers she seemed satisfied and swam back over to the other side of her enclosure and just watched us. We came back in later that night to see her again and she did the same thing all over again.

The one group of animals not looking forward to seeing us—no, they actually ignored us—were the cats. Everybody loved going to see the cats and trying to make them roar, but they just looked at us like we were idiots (very perceptive of them). They acted like they didn't have time for our shenanigans. We would do all kinds of things to get their attention—like Sonny, who one night kept waving his cap at the jaguar. It never flinched. When Sonny turned around to leave, he felt something hit him from behind. We all turned and saw the look of shock on our friend's face. The jaguar had Sonny's back pocket in his paw.

Once all of us guys dared each other to ride the giraffe, but...well, sometimes we exhibited a little common sense. We never went ahead with that crazy idea.

Throughout the fun and the festivities, Mary and I were inseparable. We loved camping and being outside and hanging around with our friends. Yet we never spoke about the son we'd given up the previous summer. For me, it was easy to compartmentalize. The drugs and the drinking made it easy to escape.

When Mary came home from Robeline, she'd told me she didn't want to have sex anymore until we got married. The silence about our baby lasted, but our vow to wait until marriage didn't. Like the drugs, it was too easy to fall back into it. Too easy and too fun.

Once Mary and I went to an older coworker's house during lunch to smoke some pot. Mary said later she didn't like going back to work being high. She was afraid somebody would find out. As for me, maybe it would have been obvious except for the fact that I was high all the time. Mary couldn't believe how often I was stoned, especially when I'd come over to her house for dinner. She always said I could hide it well, and I could. High and hungry.

Mary's mother would ask me if I wanted something to eat. Something like a chocolate malt and a roast beef sandwich, my favorites. I always said yes.

Eventually I would grow to master the art of hiding my drug use even from my dear sweet Mary. By then, the fun and the laughter would be gone.

9

IF YOU LEAVE ME NOW

LIFE is full of funny little details that stick in your memory. Like a pair of navy-blue gym shorts.

There sat Mac, my knight in shining armor, on a bench in a jail cell. He was wearing nothing but a pair of gym shorts and cowboy boots. Tired, bloodshot eyes hung under an afro that made him resemble the drummer from Grand Funk Railroad (think twenty-four inches in diameter). Mac gave me a grin, and all I wanted to do was laugh. The sight of him sitting there half-naked was hilarious. Yet I couldn't laugh, because I knew Mac was in trouble.

To be honest, we were both in trouble. Again.

It was November 1976, and Mac and I were in our freshman year at Harding University, a private Christian liberal arts college in Searcy, Arkansas, about four hours away from West Monroe. Attending Harding was somewhat of a family tradition. Most of the kids in our church ended up there.

That whole year before going off to college was a blur for me. I was exhausted from the emotional stress of having a baby and keeping it quiet, not to mention the hormonal roller coaster from my pregnancy. I worked full-time at Howard Bros. Warehouse, an office full of women. I can still hear the Teletype machine going off in our office and the ticker tape spitting out another order to be shipped out.

On the weekends Mac and I would go to the woods for big bonfires with tons of friends. On the outside I looked happy, doing my job well and socializing at the parties, but on the inside I was sad. I wondered who had our baby, what he was doing, whether he cried a lot and what that cry sounded like, what his smile looked like. I still wondered what his adopted parents had named him. It was easy to numb the pain with the constant partying, but the hurt always returned.

Going to Harding was another way to forget about our past and move on. Mac's parents wanted him to go to a Christian college. His mother had actually graduated from Abilene Christian University and wouldn't have minded him going there, but Mac followed me to Harding.

Since I'd grown up being a people pleaser, especially loving to make my dad happy, I went into college assuming I was going to be an accountant. I'd done very well in accounting in high school, so I thought I could help him take care of his businesses and manage his books. As someone who loves encouraging people on a daily basis, I know

now I would've been driven crazy if I had ended up being an accountant.

It was late on a Sunday night when I heard a knock on my dorm room door. I was surprised to find the dean of women standing in the hallway.

"Mac's been arrested," she said. "He was smoking marijuana. He's in jail and your car's been impounded. We've got to go get it."

None of this surprised me, not Mac being arrested or the fact that he was in my red Ford Mustang. I got dressed and went to the police station with the dean, who was probably startled to hear that there were a bunch of roaches found in the ashtray. I wasn't sure if she even knew the police weren't referring to bugs.

For Mac, the party at college had started earlier that summer when he took a couple of courses to get his grades up in order to be accepted. Since his classes were mostly attended by seniors, he ended up getting to know all of them and starting to party right away. By the time I showed up, he already had tons of upperclass friends who loved smoking pot and having a good time.

The irony, just one of the many interesting twists in the tight coil of our story, was that Mac's parents sent him to Harding University to straighten him out. Yet who did he meet as soon as he got onto campus? The same guy he met at Camp Idlewild in Virginia so many years before—the counselor who first introduced him to pot.

That's how Mac ended up hanging around and rooming with seniors, and we started our freshman year well entrenched in the party scene.

Two months later, it looked as though the party scene had caught up to Mac.

I drove my car back to college and Mac had to go see the dean of men in the middle of the night. The next day I heard the news.

"Cops said if the college kicks me out, the charges will be dropped."

"What happened last night anyway?"

"I never even wanted to go out," Mac told me. "I was already in bed sleeping when Donnie came over and said, 'Hey, Mac, let's go out and smoke a joint.' So I was like 'All right.' We were parked in the car smoking when the cops found us."

"So what are you going to do?"

Mac laughed. "Not much I can do. I gotta go back to Monroe."

"Then I'm going too. "

"Don't be crazy. You can't just drop out of school. Especially not you."

Mac was referring to my being an honor roll student who felt the need to excel for my family, especially my father…even if what I was studying had nothing to do with my strengths or desires.

"I'm not staying here if you're not here."

Mac knew I meant it.

A day later, after hearing the news that I was coming home, my brother called to plead with me to stay in school. Maybe my dad had put him up to it.

"There's no way you can do this," Johnny told me.

Soon the telling turned to scolding.

"You know, you're a really big disappointment to Dad and our family. There's no reason for you to come just 'cause Mac is coming home. You have to stay in school, Mary."

I might have been a people pleaser, but I was stubborn too. When it came down to doing what I wanted to do, nobody could change my mind.

"I'm coming home," I told Johnny. "I love Mac, and we want to get married. I'm coming home 'cause I want to be with him. I don't care about school."

"I can't believe you're doing this. You need to stay there and get your degree and worry about Mac later."

Even though Johnny knew about the pregnancy, he still didn't understand the connection I had with Mac. Nobody did. It was not only that we shared a history and a son we would never see again. Mac was my soul mate and best friend.

"I'm coming home," I said again.

And that's what I did.

What I didn't tell my brother was this: I thought I might be pregnant. Again.

Right before Mac got busted and expelled from Harding, I missed a period. At the time I thought, *Oh no, not again.*

There was no way I was going to go to a doctor and ask to get on the pill—I couldn't do that—yet Mac and I were messing around a lot since we were together all the time.

But I had been careful. I thought I was doing a good job of keeping track of my cycle. There was no way I could be pregnant.

This time I wasn't about to wait four months to find out. I went to the doctor as soon as I got back to Monroe and discovered it had happened. Again.

As I said, life is full of funny little details. Like that time we had sex and I might have been ovulating. Details that might get overlooked until it's too late.

Until you're pregnant, out of college, and realizing there's no turning back now.

10

BABY, I LOVE YOUR WAY

THE party was about to start. To really start. 'Cause I was finally gonna marry my soul mate.

The cool thing about being a guy is it's easy to get ready for your wedding. How long does it take to slip on a tux? So while Mary was busy at home that morning getting all pretty and ready to walk down the aisle, I was busy getting high with my best man and some other friends. Yeah, sure, I could've been a bit stressed out over the reality of the situation, but I was still having fun. I didn't need to think about our child or how I'd be able support a family or even what I was going to do with the rest of my life.

It was easy not to think about the future when I could numb the present.

By the time I showed up (late) at the church on December 27, 1976, I was totally stoned. Everybody was pretty upset at me, especially my parents, but I was good at acting the part and making everybody laugh. Mary was just excited to see me and finally do what we had wanted to do for the last year.

It was kinda crazy how quickly everything had happened, from my getting kicked out of school to discovering Mary was pregnant. I remember well our conversation with Mary's father.

"We're getting married," we told him.

Of course, considering our age and that we had dropped out of college, Mary's father didn't like this idea.

"I'm pregnant again," Mary said.

"Okay—you're getting married now!"

Three weeks later, boom. Here we were on our wedding day.

I was once again amazed at how Alton Howard treated Mary and me in a kind and gentle manner. He never made us feel guilty or ashamed. I see now the Christlike example he was setting for us, though at the time I didn't pay much attention to that sort of thing.

Mary told her parents she didn't want them spending a lot of money on the wedding, but that didn't stop them from going all out as if they'd been planning it for six months.

I'd like to say that I remember every single moment of that day, from the time I first saw my beautiful bride walking down the aisle to the moment we gave our vows and promised to love each other for the rest of our lives. I'd love to describe the moment we kissed, when I knew I was finally going to grow up and be a man and take some responsibility in my life. But I was flying high and loving life and all I really remember was I couldn't wait for the party to begin.

Everything up till now was dress rehearsal. I was ready to take my partner and split and get on the road. Like a modern-day Bonnie and Clyde.

Rice rained over our heads, but it felt like relief. We were leaving the church and our families to get to where we really wanted to be.

The real party was waiting when we arrived at our new home, a 70-by-14-foot trailer. All the trailers in the park were end to end instead of side by side, so we had a yard and we backed up to the woods. The front door led into the den, with the kitchen to the immediate left and bedrooms on either side. I'd put Klipsch La Scala speakers—three feet tall and two feet deep—in each of the bedrooms. Let me tell you, whenever we listened to music, the walls would shake.

The trailer had a woodsy, Western theme, and to us it felt like the Taj Mahal. All of our friends were there waiting, and the party had started a long time before we arrived. We let all the neighbors know we were there. Music blasted from a big stereo with a stack of albums ready to play all night.

One song we played and danced to that summed up how I felt was Doug Kershaw's "It Takes All Day." Try listening to this song without bobbing your head and tapping your feet. As the fiddles played, Mary and I laughed and sang and embraced this magical thing called *marriage*. At one point I was somehow convinced that getting on top of the coffee table to dance would be a good thing.

Everybody was drunk and high and having the time of their lives. These were the people that mattered, the people who understood us. Near the end of the party, we told all our friends good night. Tomorrow Mary and I were heading out on our honeymoon, though we didn't have a thing planned. We were just going to get in the car and see how far we could go on the cash we'd received as wedding gifts.

We slept in after the late night, so we left a little after lunch. We'd been driving for a while when we passed a long-haired drifter hitchhiking on the side of the highway.

"Let's pick him up," I said.

I didn't think that much about it. Sure, the guy smelled a bit, and he looked like he might have escaped from the local prison, but it was all good. Mary sat in the front seat next to me while our hitchhiker sat in the back. My new bride gave me a few worried looks, but the stranger seemed friendly enough to me. He even offered me some of his pot, which was cool.

An hour into our wedding trip, I'm smoking dope with a stranger while my beautiful bride is poking me on the leg. After a little while I came up with an excuse to get him out of our car.

"Hey, man, you know—we got this family thing we have to go to, so we better let you out."

Maybe I could have just told him it was our *honeymoon*... but eventually we were alone again.

Mary turned to me with a serious look. "If you want this to be a good honeymoon, don't ever pull that stunt again."

We hadn't even been married for twenty-four hours, and my wife was already giving me good marital advice.

Maybe we should've planned ahead, but back then I wasn't exactly the planning type. Remember? I'm the guy who showed up late for the wedding. When we arrived in Shreveport, all of the hotels were sold out because of a new racetrack called Louisiana Downs that had opened recently. So we had to turn around and drive sixty miles back to Ruston. I think we passed the same hitchhiker on the way back. I guess we were the only ones who gave him a ride.

Finding a hotel in Ruston was just as difficult. We finally found a run-down place to stay, but neither of us cared. We had all we needed.

Room service the next morning was me slipping out and bringing Mary breakfast in bed from the Huddle House. Only the best for my new bride.

So I was young and pretty stupid, but I felt like the king of the world. We only had a couple of days to enjoy being newlyweds since I was starting a new job in the warehouse of Howard Bros. Discount Store. I wasn't thinking very far ahead; I was living in the moment. And the moment meant Mary. The moment meant she was finally by my side. Like the bright morning sun, things were going to be good.

11

SHOW ME THE WAY

I can still see the girl carrying her shame and sadness all by herself.

Am I to blame? the girl asks herself at the start of a new year. *Am I the cause of this?*

A new year begins, but the same old questions haunt her.

What will my family think?

The same fears burn.

Did worry make me miscarry?

The same guilt hovers.

The nineteen-year-old tells only her new husband and her father what has happened.

Is God punishing me just like He did with those doctors and nurses the moment I delivered our son?

The new bride knows the honeymoon is over.

Can God take this pain...this shame...and wash it away?

The expecting mother is no longer expecting.

The girl now wonders if she will forever carry the pain and the scars around with her.

How will I ever fill these two holes inside of me?

Yes, I can still see that girl.

I know, in time, she will learn the answers to her questions. But not in the way she might expect.

12

FLY LIKE AN EAGLE

SOME friends celebrate when you graduate from college. Ours celebrated the fact that I'd been tossed out.

I didn't have to go far to find the party. Oftentimes, the party found me.

Take, for instance, the time right after I'd gotten kicked out of college, when Mary and I went to Arkansas to see some friends. Over fifty people were ready and waiting on us to go out into the country and party.

Well, this was the first time I ever drank gin. We headed out into the country and we're drinking gin and we finally got to the place where we were going to party. It was at a waterfall, a really cool place. We had to walk to the cars, about a mile, to get stuff and bring it back to where we were going to camp. It was late at night and dark and it started pouring down rain. Somewhere between the camp-site and the car, I got lost and passed out in the middle of a cow pasture. When I woke up, I was still drunk on the gin and didn't have a clue where I was.

I finally made it back to where everybody was partying. "Where have you been?" everyone asked.

"I don't know, but let me help you build this fire." So I started working on the fire. Still drunk. There was a guy splitting wood nearby who accidently hit me in the head with the ax. It hurt, but I was so drunk I didn't think much about it. Yeah, just another ax cracking my head. No big deal.

I woke up the next morning with half an afro. On the other side of my head, the hair and skull were solid dried blood. Maybe I should've checked that the night before—you know, *after being hit with an ax.* But nah. I was fine. Mary likes to joke that I didn't get killed because I had so much hair to cushion the blow. Maybe it's not a joke. I still have a crease in my head today.

The cut didn't knock any sense into me, however. The wounds would have to go a lot deeper to do that.

Now just because I'd been kicked out of college and liked partying and smoking pot didn't mean I wasn't willing to work hard. Perhaps I got my strong work ethic from my military father. Every morning I got up at five, and before going to work at the Howard Bros. Discount store, I would drive to the labor hall and hope my name would get called. I had heard you could go to this labor pool and they would send you out to work in a mill where you'd make six bucks an hour. *Six bucks, for doing what? Digging ditches and stuff? Are you kidding?* We thought that was big money at the time, so I said, "Sign me up."

After just a few days I got called out, and I never did show back up for Howard Bros. Since it was a labor union, they took $168 out of my first week's pay for union dues. I was a laborer for a year and made good friends with some carpenters who got me into the carpenters' union as an apprentice.

That was the start of my career as a cabinetmaker. That's what I had wanted to do all the time, anyway, since taking shop in the seventh grade. I made my first bookshelf that year, and I still have it today.

For the next four years I worked as an apprentice carpenter, going around to different jobs and learning the business. I worked very hard perfecting my craft. I also continued to perfect my other craft: partying.

There was never a letup. If we weren't partying in the trailer park, we'd go party in Arkansas. For variety we'd go pick mushrooms. Just as in building cabinets, there's an art at picking the right mushrooms. You want to eat the ones that will make you high, as opposed to, say, the ones that will kill you. So we were really good at picking the right mushrooms out of cow patties.

That's right—cow patties.

After a really heavy dew or rain, we'd go out in search of psilocybin mushrooms and boil them down in Kool-Aid. It actually makes you real sick at first, but within fifteen minutes of that upset stomach you have an uncontrollable grin on your face. The high would last all night long, twelve hours or more.

Mary never cared for any of that stuff. She tried mushrooms a few times, but they scared her because of the hallucinations. No drug ever scared me enough to keep away from it.

Even though Mary and I were both working, people would always be coming to our trailer to party. Sometimes we would say, “Look, we’re going to bed; y’all leave when you want to.” Everybody was having a good time and we didn’t want to end it, even if we had to get sleep for the coming day.

One night we had already gone to bed when we heard stuff flying around inside our trailer in the other room.

I slipped out of bed and opened the door. My buddy Dane, one of my closest friends, was standing there totally naked, taking the knobs off the stereo and throwing them around the trailer. Obviously he was a bit high on those magical mushrooms.

“What are you doing, man?” I asked.

“I got to get all this stuff out of here,” Dane said as if the stereo were possessed.

“I’ll tell you who’s getting out of here.” I picked him up, threw him out the door, and closed it. And yeah, he was still totally naked. Mary and I went back to bed. Next thing we knew, we saw the reflections of cop lights in our bedroom.

Oh no.

When I looked outside, I saw the police car coming down our driveway and Dane standing at the next-door neighbor's trailer, buck naked, banging on the door. He must have spotted the cop lights too, because he suddenly took off. The cops chased after him. Obviously our neighbor had called after seeing a naked guy knocking at their door.

Mary and I decided to lie low and keep the lights off, and the cops never even knocked on our door. Mary told me later she was praying the cops wouldn't come to our trailer. She asked God to get us out of this trouble and promised we'd never do something like this again.

Just one more time, God. Yeah, one more time.

I think those prayers got prayed a lot back then, and even though we didn't deserve it, God answered a lot of them.

The next morning I went outside and spotted Dane sitting in his truck, just waiting there. I walked over to him.

"Man, what were you thinking last night?"

"Don't even go there, man, 'cause I don't know," Dane said. "All I know is I woke up in a briar patch out here this morning. I am cut up."

There he sat in his truck, still totally naked, cut up from head to toe, wincing in pain.

"I can't move right now, man, and I don't know what happened and I don't want to talk about it."

Being the sort of friend that I am, we never talked about that again. Not a word.

But the party still raged. And so did I.

13

YOU MAKE LOVING FUN

I grew up in a home where my mom cooked three meals a day and we sat down at the table for each meal together. Well—that was on the days when Mom was doing okay. So after Mac and I got married, I felt like I was playing house, having my own place to take care of. I loved cooking him breakfast. I would fix our lunches for work the day before and then come home to prepare a home-cooked supper. Mac's favorite was fried pork chops, real mashed potatoes, and homemade biscuits with gravy—real southern fare.

I decided to keep working instead of going back to college. I couldn't afford to put myself through school, and I wasn't going to ask my dad for any more money—he'd already paid for having the baby and all kinds of things. Since my father needed somebody in the office at the jewelry store, I went to work there.

During that time, our home was the place to be. Friends came over every evening, and we either listened to music in our trailer or went outside in the woods for a bonfire. We always had the energy for a party. On the weekends the guys would stay up all night setting out trotlines and catch a boatload of crappie, and the next weekend we'd have a big fish fry. There were no mean drunks and nobody gossiped about anybody else. There was never any anger or negativity, only fun times doing crazy and funny things.

The church crowd I had grown up with, on the other hand, were judgmental and constantly gossiped. Their rules seemed very strict and superficial. I knew a lot of kids who drank and partied on the weekend and then sat in church on Sunday.

At our parties, nobody tried to be anything they weren't. I felt at home. I felt accepted. And because everybody else was partying just like me, I felt free of shame. At least for the moment.

I still thought about the son Mac and I had given up. Smoking pot helped to numb the pain of wondering where he was. I no longer had to worry about my father finding out what I was doing. We were with friends who were safe. But I did think about God, knowing I was disappointing Him. Though the partying temporarily covered up my sadness, the pain was still there, along with something else.

Guilt.

I knew who God was and had since I was a child. I knew He didn't like the choices I was making or the home we were building. Soon it became difficult to have a fun time.

The partying and the smoking and all of that were not part of a good Christian home, the kind of home I wanted our children to be raised in.

The longing for a more stable home began to grow inside of me. So one day, I'd had enough. It was like I finally knew I needed to grow up; the party needed to end. I didn't know anything about addiction. I just said, "I'm not doing it anymore," and I quit.

For some people, it's that easy.

My conversation with Mac went something like this:

"Let's have a baby," I said.

Laid-back Mac nodded and said, "All right, that'd be cool."

"But I'm going to stop doing all this partying."

Mac nodded again. "Well, go ahead. I'm not."

I could tell there was no negotiating, not with Mac. But at the time I was fine with it. *He'll come around,* I thought. *He'll eventually stop, just like me.*

Since it seemed like we could both blink and I'd be pregnant, a baby was soon on the way. For a while I stayed away from the partying. But loneliness set in, and our old friends kept saying, "Mary, come on back."

So I still attended parties. I was the only pregnant, sober person there.

The good news for everybody was that we had a consistent designated driver.

Back then most of our parties were held outside, but every now and then we went out to a bar. One night as we were driving home after midnight, three cars were racing back to our house. We were all going extremely fast, passing each other on the Cheniere Dam. We didn't give the approaching car any notice until we saw that it was a sheriff. As he passed us, he realized how fast we all were going and immediately turned on his lights. But he was going the opposite direction and couldn't turn around on the narrow dam. It took him an extra few minutes to get headed in our direction. We never let up in speed, knowing he was coming and thinking we could get away.

Mac and I were in the rear of the three cars, because of course I was the only one sober. Mac hooted and hollered, telling me to go faster. We turned down the road to our house, knowing we only had a mile to go and would be in our safe haven. Our friends in the other cars had already raced down our driveway, parked at the edge of the woods, gotten out, and run down to the lake at the bottom of the hill to hide.

I pulled up in our driveway, and Mac said to stop in front of our house. He got out and leaned against the back of our car waiting on the cops. He looked cool and calm, while I sat in the driver's seat about to have a heart attack.

Sure enough, here came the cops, lights blazing and siren wailing.

"What can I do for you officers?" Mac asked after they got out of their cars.

"We think you guys are driving drunk," the sheriff said. "Where are the other two vehicles?"

They hadn't had time to clock our speed, so they didn't know exactly how fast we were going. Mac, well accustomed to run-ins with the law, simply smiled and spoke in his charming way.

"I'm sorry, officers. My wife was driving this car. She doesn't drink, and there's nobody else with us."

Eventually the cops left. It took us about an hour to find our friends because they were so well hidden and too scared to come out.

We had a lot of stories like that, funny stories fueled by our age and by drugs and alcohol. Our family of friends had this camaraderie partying. As long as we kept it a secret, we could have all the fun we wanted. Life was full of everything beautiful, we thought. It was full of romance, fun, and adventure.

Yet Mac and I had our own secrets that we never discussed with anyone else, not even each other. We had two babies we would never know. One baby whose name and address we didn't know and the other in heaven.

I thought life would change once we finally had a baby of our own, a baby we finally would keep. And it did.

Mac's partying only got worse.

14

ALREADY GONE

EVEN back then, God was seeking me out.

You can run but you can't hide.

But I didn't want to listen. I only wanted to turn up the volume of my life louder.

You think you can find me, God? I'm just going to turn up David Gilmour's guitar solo and smoke a little pot and hide out.

I also wanted to get away from the Pharisees and the phonies I saw all the time. I wanted to be secluded and isolated so Mary and I could live our own lives without anybody judging us. I just wanted to have a good time, and I didn't want God or anybody else interfering with that plan.

That's how we ended up on Cheniere Lake.

"Come on, let's go check it out."

When I first told Mary's father about my desire for a secluded place to build a house, he mentioned some acreage he'd bought years ago on Cheniere Lake.

But I could see the uncertainty on Mary's face as we stood on the property for the first time. We could have easily bought a nice little house in the nice little subdivision where the rest of our family lived. But the idea of living in a place like that, surrounded by family…I told Mary that wasn't for me. I always thought it'd be cool to live on a lake surrounded by woods and wildlife and water.

So there we were, checking out this heavily wooded plot of land my father-in-law had guided us to.

You could barely go ten feet without coming across a dogwood just coming into bloom. None of the trees had their leaves yet, so the entire woods looked covered in snow. Right behind them were wild azaleas that were bright pink, perfectly accenting the sea of white. I knew at once which trees I shouldn't cut down. We needed to keep this beautiful sight.

The 3.6 acres seemed more like a thousand to us. As we walked through briars and bushes, Mary and I scoured the ground, watching for water moccasins. The land sloped downward toward the lake, but we couldn't see it since the trees and brush were so dense. Squirrels jumped around us from tree to tree. Birds sang and crickets chirped and frogs croaked. You couldn't hear any cars or see a sign of anything other than wildlife.

When we got to the bottom and saw the beautiful lake hidden like a diamond in the rough, I knew this was the place we needed to be. Our backyard would be four thousand acres of swampland. It was the perfect place to get away and enjoy the wildlife. Both nature's and ours.

I looked at Mary. "Think about all the fishing and hunting and bonfires we could have."

"There's no road on this land," she said.

"We'll make one."

It was a dream come true for us to have our own land. We couldn't get the deal signed quickly enough, I was so eager to start cutting a path in for our trailer. I didn't want to put it right on the road; I wanted to place it way back in so we could see the lake from our window and have privacy. So I bought a Homelite chain saw and an old Massey Ferguson tractor and began carving a path into the woods for our new homestead. The driveway had to be just right. It couldn't be just straight in; it had to have some curves. It also had to miss the biggest oak trees, though we had to cut some to have a place to put our trailer.

On weekends we went out to the property to cut down trees and make a path, and eventually we moved the trailer there. A year later, right around the time Mary became pregnant, I started building the house.

I would work all day in construction, then come home and work until dark on the house. Whenever I was in between construction jobs, I worked on it as well. It took about a year to build the shell. We moved in and continued to finish it...a lifetime project. I was always thinking of something new to do to our home—like the time I cut down a cypress tree and shaved off all the bark and turned it into a door casing in our den. Over the years I built many pieces, not only for Mary but for family and friends.

We didn't know what was ahead and frankly, I didn't care. I just wanted to be with Mary and away from everybody else. I wanted to have fun adventures tromping through the woods and going out on the lake. I wanted to count the number of stars in the skies and sit around a fire beneath them without a worry. I had hopes for a good life together.

Yeah—high hopes. The kind of hopes fueled by a man constantly high.

The kind that usually don't turn out so pretty.

15

SONGBIRD

THE moment I touched our little girl for the first time, I knew the gift God had given to us. Yet I also realized anew the grave mistake we had made.

It was April 3, 1980, and Mac was standing by my bedside. The waiting room down the hall was full of family. Our friends were wondering when they'd hear news of the birth. I was wide awake, out of breath, and full of an indescribable joy only a new mother seeing her baby for the first time could feel. It was the sensation of holding in my arms this beautiful, tiny child I'd carried so long.

But the realization hit me like a tsunami.

We gave up our firstborn baby. A baby just like this. A baby who would've been her big brother.

I trembled under the weight of immense joy and pain.

From the time I was little, my father, who gave everyone nicknames, had called me his little Cherry Berry. While I was pregnant, Mac and I went back and forth with names. Even by the time she was born, we still hadn't decided what to call her. But when we first saw her—a head full of curly wet hair, rosy round chubby cheeks, and the sweetest eyes I had ever seen—Mac instantly knew the perfect name. "Let's call her Cherry!"

I studied her tiny fingers, her round nose, her soft skin. All with this surreal feeling of being given the most amazing gift ever, and with the sinking feeling that I'd given a gift just like that away.

And I'll never get him back. Never.

I was holding my baby and she was perfect. She breathed and gurgled next to me. She had a face and a name. She had a father and a mother looking over her and loving her.

And somewhere she has a brother who will never, ever know her.

My tears were truly bittersweet. From one eye came a tear of pure thankfulness, from the other a tear of shame. They lined my cheeks and were joined by others as emotions I'd kept hidden and buried finally came unleashed.

My doctor looked at me with confusion on his face. "What's the matter?" he asked.

I probably looked like a crazy woman because I was crying so hard.

He consoled me like a calm parent of a sobbing toddler. "You have a beautiful, healthy baby girl. There's nothing wrong with her."

He didn't know our story. There was no way he could understand my emotions.

"I'll put her back in if you want me to," he joked.

I smiled and shook my head and said, "No, no, I'm okay."

I never explained the truth to our doctor. Once he left Mac and me alone, I looked up with tears still filling my eyes.

"How did we give our baby up?" I asked in a faint voice. "Her brother...How did we give him up? Look what we gave up."

I had never understood the bond between a mother and a child, a bond that had been cut as quickly as an umbilical cord. For so long I had been missing something, this thing that I couldn't describe or didn't even know. But now I knew exactly what it was. I held it in my arms.

Cherry began to cry, and I tried to soothe her. Then I remembered I'd never heard our son's cry. Not even once.

God gave Mac and me a blessing even when we didn't deserve it. That's the way He often works. I carried around the guilt and shame of giving up our firstborn, and God knew that. It was like He said, *Okay, I'm going to take care of you two because I love you.* And in our hands He placed sweet Cherry.

Her disposition matched her beautiful looks. The nurses loved playing beauty salon with the thick locks she inherited from her father. Each time they brought her to me, they'd have her hair styled a different way! I felt like a queen lying in that hospital bed. Each time they placed Cherry in my arms, it was like I was receiving a gift, and each time I held her in amazement.

But Mac and I couldn't truly appreciate the blessing God had given us in Cherry back then. We were still in the early chapters of our tale. In a lot of ways, it turned out we were each telling a very different story in our increasingly different lives.

It would take another gift and blessing from God to get us back on the same page.

16

COMFORTABLY NUMB

THIS is what it's like to be a slave to an addiction.

There is only one war story, and it's the same for every addict: it's the need for more. But you're different. You're not like them. You don't have a problem. You'll be okay.

Yeah, sure, you've been using since you were twelve. You were just a kid when a camp counselor said, "Hey, man, I got some stuff here you might want to try." You were curious and already smoked cigarettes and grown-ups said *that* would kill you and it hadn't, so how bad could it be? The counselor said, "It's like cigarettes, but man, it'll make you feel really good."

So you tried it and you sure felt it and you sure liked it. It was an escape when you felt scrutinized so much.

Drinking was never your thing, not really, but smoking dope sure was. The party never stopped. The drugs never ran out. High school. College (the brief blink that it was). Marriage. Babies.

For you life just keeps staying cool. Far out and far enough away not to hinder your habits.

Besides, these people around you are real. They aren't phonies. They aren't Pharisees. These people will be your friends for the rest of your life. They *get* you. They *know* you.

You work hard, so you deserve to shake off the dust of the day and let loose. Live a little. Party a little. Fish and hunt and hang out and listen to music and feel good. Go up. Fly high.

So yeah, sure, your wife isn't partying anymore, so she's not around as much. She's pregnant, and that's cool. Yeah. That's all good. She's stopped smoking, but you're not about to stop. Having a child doesn't scare you. It's not going to make you change.

It didn't the first time you found out. Or the second time.

You're still young and having a good time and living for the moment.

You tell yourself drinking and smoking pot are fine.

So it's that easy to say yes when something new is offered.

"Want some speed?"

You feel young and fun and invincible and you don't give it a second thought.

Sweet Mary isn't around. You never think that maybe you shouldn't.

Why not?

You've tried a lot of heavy drugs. But you don't like the ones that bring you down. If you're going to do something, you want to go up.

You like speed because you can stay up as long as you want and do other drugs. This also means you can drink as much as you want to, even though alcohol isn't really your deal.

So you try it and realize this is different. This changes everything.

All you can think is one sweet thing.

Where has this been my whole life?

Yeah, it's that good. You're not going to lie. You love it.

And nothing—absolutely nothing—feels as good as this sweet ride upward. It stirs your heart and your soul. You feel fantastic.

Yeah.

This isn't some shadowy corner you find yourself standing in. This isn't some dark side of the moon. This is the sweet spot of the sun, and you don't want to leave.

After trying crystal meth for the first time, you never want to leave this summit that's so high and so beautiful.

17

TRY JUST A LITTLE BIT HARDER

MOTHERHOOD was everything I imagined it would be. Yet in many ways I felt like a single parent.

Cherry was born in 1980, and Callie followed three years later. I had our girls in everything. They started violin when they were three years old. They were in gymnastics, T-ball, soccer, basketball—whatever the sport was for that season, the girls did it. We'd often go over to my parents' house. They had a lake behind the house where the kids would go fishing or just play with their mamaw and papaw. I was constantly doing something with them that kept us away from the house.

Looking back, I understand why.

Mac and I were living separate lives at that point. Yet I never knew the full truth behind how different our lives really were. It wasn't like Mac had suddenly become a vegetable who sat around the house all day smoking pot and eating Cheetos. By the time Callie was born, he had opened the M&M Millworks cabinet shop on our property. Business was good and he stayed busy.

And Mac loved those little girls. He was with me in the delivery room at both of their births. When the girls were babies, he would hold them, feed them bottles, rock them, and sing to them. He read stories to them at night before they went to bed. They loved their daddy. He was a fun daddy and he loved to make them laugh. As they got older, he attended everything they were involved in: T-ball games, violin recitals, gymnastic meets, basketball games…He was there and was just as high as a kite, but nobody knew that except me. It was like his normal now.

During our early days as parents, Mac still smoked pot in the house. When the girls would go to bed, we would have friends over and they would smoke in the den. Several of our friends were cigarette smokers, so our girls didn't know the difference. Mac was careful not to smoke around them, pot or cigarettes. He would either go outside, smoke at the shop during work, or wait until they had gone to bed.

We always had loud music going in those huge Klipsch speakers. There were still lots of parties down the hill by the lake, where the guys would fish all night with rock-and-roll music jamming through the woods.

M&M Millworks was thriving. Mac loved to work in his shop and always had more jobs than he could keep up with. He would create beautiful pieces of furniture for us and for customers. Eventually it got to where he was at the shop more than he was at the house.

The more he was absent, the more I got involved at the girls' school. I was always the room mother and went on all their field trips, along with saying yes to anything anybody asked me to do at school or church. I led the children's Christmas program, taught in Bible classes, hosted wedding and baby showers in our home, went to ladies' Bible studies, and became the crafts director at the summer camp where Mac and I met.

I went over to my parents' house daily just to be around positive surroundings. The girls would feed the ducks, go fishing, play with cousins, and dance and sing with a microphone while my dad played the piano or guitar. My mom would let them make a huge mess in the kitchen creating all kinds of food concoctions. We stayed so busy away from home that by the time we would get back, it was time to eat and have the girls go to bed.

I still loved Mac, and we still did stuff together like going on camping trips and taking the girls on various excursions. I kept thinking that if I just did enough things right, our marriage would turn into something good.

I never told anybody about his smoking because I knew they would just make Mac angry, so I began to simply pray for him all the time. The Bible verse that came to mind as I began praying and never stopping was Romans 8:28: "And we know that in all things God works for the good of those who love him, who have been called according to his purpose." I kept this verse in my thoughts and recited it to remind myself. Even when things turned dark and the days tilted toward despair, I kept praying to God for Mac.

I needed to keep my faith and hope and trust in God, not just for myself or for Cherry or Callie. I needed to keep it for Mac, for his well-being. And as it turned out, to help keep him alive.

I had mastered the art of keeping family secrets. First there was my mother with her illness that nobody ever talked about. Then there was the baby Mac and I had given up. Now it was Mac's drug addiction.

So we would go to church and pretend like everybody in our family was okay.

I had hoped that Mac would eventually stop just like I had. I assumed that having Cherry and Callie would be two giant wake-up calls to get his act together. But it's not always that easy, and some people need to learn the hard way.

I remember when the lady who came to clean the house once a month found Mac asleep in the family room with a big bag of dope right next to him. She brought it to me and asked what it was. I wasn't sure what to tell her, so I went to Mac and asked him what to say.

"Tell her the neighbor kids built a fort next door and I found it in there," Mac said.

It wasn't just a lie, it was a good lie, and he had come up with it on the spot. He had mastered the art of deception and I didn't even realize it.

When I told the woman what Mac said, she shook her head and looked concerned. "Wow, I hope he gets some help."

For a second I thought she was talking about Mac. Then I realized she was referring to the kid who had left the marijuana in the fort.

I'm living with that grown-up kid in a fort he built himself, I thought, *and he's not about to get any help.*

That grown-up kid wanted his bag back, however. And I gave in like I always did.

But the more I gave in, and the more time passed, the more Mac seemed to change. Something was wrong. He was gone so much of the time, but when he was around, there were times when he acted truly insane. I didn't know what was going on, and I figured it was just marijuana and alcohol. I knew he occasionally experimented with some other things, but I didn't know he was using on a regular basis.

I put on a smile and stayed busy and kept our pretty little girls occupied. I kept working and kept praying and kept trying just a little bit harder. Meanwhile, our home and our family were disintegrating before my very eyes. Selfishly—and foolishly—I tried to keep the rest of the world's eyes from seeing how broken we had become.

God knew, however. God knew everything.

18

TIGHTROPE

THAT fun-loving kid I used to be was gone. But the husband and father and man I should have become never showed up. In his place was this creature that wanted and needed only one thing. I was a modern-day Gollum, constantly on the search for his "precious." Nobody else knew, not even Mary. There was one thing that drove me, and that was why on this day I steered my car through the neighborhood to a house I'd come to know so well.

My eyes scanned the streets to make sure I wasn't being followed. Just to make sure nobody was paying any attention to this little nondescript house. Inside was a little nondescript person who wasn't my friend. He was a means to an end. And that end—a brutal, cold, and lonely end—seemed like a shadow pulling me closer as the days passed.

I pulled the car in front of the house and shut off the engine.

I glanced down the driveway, then across the street, then up ahead, then back again. Maybe once or twice or a dozen times. I felt the 9mm Beretta tucked in my jeans. This wasn't a Dirty Harry movie, because if it was, I would have been on the opposite side of his .44 Magnum being asked whether I felt lucky.

No, I didn't feel lucky anymore. I just felt want. I felt need. I wanted and needed another ounce of meth because *that's* what made me feel lucky. Running out wasn't an option. Not anymore.

Before opening the door, I looked at the two sweet faces of my daughters in the backseat. I had just picked them up from their grandparents, and they waited for me now, smiling and wondering why I had parked the car.

"I'll be back in just a minute," I told them.

They were safe, I told myself, because I was watching out for them. I was taking care of them.

I'd take care of business and then leave and everything would still be perfect. Just like it always was.

Just like it always would be.

I didn't just blink and suddenly find myself addicted to meth. I worked long and hard to graduate to this level of addiction. Yet even after that first time of snorting it at a party one night, when I simply thought it was speed, I set limits for myself. One limit was saying I'd never use a needle. Needles had always made me a little squeamish. Only real drug addicts used needles.

For about a year I used meth on a recreational basis. I didn't have a constant stash of it, though anytime I found it, I was quick to get some. By the end of the year I had grown to love the long-lasting effect the drug had on me. I could stay high up to twelve hours. Soon I made it a point to never be out of it.

Once at a party a friend had some meth and asked if I could help him out. He and his girlfriend wanted me to shoot them up; for some reason they thought I could do that.

"Sure I can," I lied.

At that point in my life lying was as common as breathing or smoking pot or blinking. I did it so often that it had become just the normal way to react. I didn't realize that being a drug addict also meant being a con man. I was both and did both very well.

After shooting them up, I saw firsthand the immediate rush and effect they got.

Wow, that might be worth trying.

Yeah, sure, it involved needles, but it worked really, really well. So I found out where to buy needles and for the next couple of days got somebody to shoot me up. I liked it. It was an immediate, almost-debilitating, overwhelming attack on my whole system.

Which sounds horrible but it's actually awesome, so yeah, let's attack the whole system a little more!

Suddenly pot seemed like seventh-grade silliness.

This is the real deal and yeah I'm pricking my arm a bit and injecting a poison into my system but whatever.

So that's how it happened. Doing this thing I had promised myself I'd never, ever do. Doing it over and over, numerous times a day. Doing it all the time. Living and breathing and longing for it.

But I had everything under control. This actually helped me out, I thought, because it helped me work and focus and forget about things like sleep and the woman I married and the girls we lived with and every good thing God had given me.

Everything under control?

Yeah, right.

"I thought we had more money in our account."

It was the tenth of the month, and Mary and I were arguing. Again.

"I probably forgot to deposit a check or something," I said.

Another lie.

I could see the concern on her face. The questioning in her eyes.

"What? What do you think I'm doing? Stealing from myself?"

"I've gone through these bills three times," she said. "It's like we're missing something."

This happened around the same time every month. Mary would do the bills and notice that we didn't have as much money as she assumed we did. She was right, of course. She had no idea that a nice chunk of that money was going up my arm and into my bloodstream.

"What do you want me to say?" I asked her.

Sometimes I'd ignore the questions and sometimes I'd make something up. Sometimes I'd be too tired to answer her, so I'd stay gone. Sometimes I'd get angry and turn against her.

"You just work so hard, so I'm surprised—"

"Yeah, I'm surprised too," I interrupted.

I was angry and didn't want to be bothered. I was busy and we had bills to pay and how *dare* she question me? How dare she?

Robert De Niro would have been proud of my performance.

Sometimes we'd have brutal arguments that lasted a long time. I never thought about hitting her—never. I knew she'd take off if I did. But I fought back and always managed to get through the tenth of the month, and then it would be smooth sailing once more. Enough energy to build a skyscraper while I whittled away at the ounce of meth in my pocket and the ounce of hope in my soul.

I never saw spiders crawling up the wall or coming to eat me, but I always thought there were cops right around the corner ready to bust me. I only trusted people I knew or had grown up with. I didn't want to be introduced to anybody new at this point in my life. At one time there were three main people I got drugs from, two of them heavily addicted to meth themselves. The problem with these two was that they were out of it sometimes, so they weren't very dependable. As if, in my mind, a drug addict *could* actually be dependable.

Sometimes they wouldn't come to the door. Once when I realized a dealer was in his house but wouldn't answer the door, I went to a convenience store's pay phone and called his number. I set the receiver on top of the phone and left to go back to his house. There was no such thing as caller ID or answering machines in those days. When I got back to his house, I could hear the phone ringing. After about an hour, I could see him as he walked by a window while I was sitting in the driveway in my car. Of course he was wondering what idiot was trying to call him. And of course it wasn't me because I was sitting in the driveway.

See, I still had my wits about me.

Another time I drove around the block about fifty times waiting to see if anybody would come out of his house. I just kept riding around, watching, waiting, worrying about whether I'd get another ounce or not.

The sun rose and set with me thinking this way. The sun needed its rest but I didn't. Not on the drug.

Heaven forbid I ever got off it.

I never got delusional. Yes, I had heard you could get AIDS from dirty needles. And yes, I believed I could get this dreaded disease from the clean needles only I used. Nobody else thought or said this, but I knew it in my heart. But no, I wasn't delusional. I was thinking more clearly that I ever had before in my life…

I need to be careful with these things.

That's called paranoia.

No, I just don't want to get AIDS.

But what about the time you didn't have a needle, so you used Frank's after cleaning it with some alcohol?

I never did that. Well, I only did it once.

That last needle you used was blunt and felt like you were putting a stick in your arm.

Yeah, okay, but I was almost always safe and always took good care of myself.

What about the time when Mary grabbed your arm after coming out of the movie and you winced?

Whatever, leave me alone. Why am I talking to myself anyway?

Because I can convince you of anything, can't I, long-lost buddy friend pal.

I ran around most of the time knowing I was losing my mind but so busy looking for drugs, I didn't mind it being gone.

Sleep came on occasions. Like on Sunday mornings when Mary dragged me to church. Sometimes I'd still need to use the restroom and shoot up there when I needed a pickup. Other times I'd finally get a little sleep slouched in the pew, then would get out of there as fast as possible.

Once after church Mary said to me, "Mac, what do you think is going to happen if you die? I mean, do you think you're going to heaven? You know, the way you're living?"

"I don't want to talk about it," I said.

I didn't.

If she only really knew.

But if I had been totally honest with her, I would have said this: "Yeah, I know where I'm going, and it's not heaven. But I have plenty of time to change my ways... later. I'm still young."

But questions like that—thoughts about where I was going to spend eternity and all that...please. Those weren't even in the equation. The only thing that mattered, more than God and Jesus and heaven and hell and Mary and Cherry and Callie, was getting the next high.

So while continuing to run up these steps searching for that higher ground, I didn't realize I was really sprinting down them toward a dark and dreary dungeon.

Its name was death.

In truth, an entire book could be written about those dark days. A book of brutal war stories.

Imagine the worst place you've ever been. Can you remember?

That's all you need to know about those days.

But know this, too. The light is always brighter when you've been stuck in the dark for so long. I'm not proud of all the scars I created in those shadows, yet I share them because of the shining grace that saved me and kept me alive.

19

STORMS

DARKNESS surrounded me no matter what time of day it was and no matter how clear the heavens might be. I felt like I was wading in the grime and the muck of the lake behind us, cold and wet and deserted, hanging on to a life preserver. So many nights I would cry myself to sleep. And all I'd think about was the psalm where David spoke about that.

You keep track of all my sorrows.

My sorrows clung around me even as I tried to outrun them with Cherry and Callie. They took my breath away even as I put on a good face and smiled and acted the part of the good wife and the happy mother.

You have collected all my tears in your bottle.

Every single hope that I had in my heart, every one that daily went unheard and unseen...I believed God saw them and knew them.

You have recorded each one in your book.

If I hadn't thought this, I would have lost my mind the same way I thought Mac was losing his. I couldn't do enough and control enough and say enough.

I was powerless.

Nothing—*nothing*—was in my control.

Never give up, the verse told me.

I tried not to.

Though our bodies are dying, our spirits are being renewed every day.

I felt like I was dying, but I did everything I could to cling on to the life preserver of Scripture and to the saving grace of prayer.

Our present troubles are small and won't last very long. Yet they produce for us a glory that vastly outweighs them and will last forever!

These weren't words to recite out of duty. They were staples keeping my open wounds together. They were stitches keeping my insides from falling out.

So we don't look at the troubles we can see now; rather, we fix our gaze on things that cannot be seen. For the things we see now will soon be gone, but the things we cannot see will last forever.

I still believed there was hope, though I couldn't see a single trace of it. No sign of life coming through to rescue me out of this watery hole. No semblance of Mac ever getting over whatever was happening to him.

No visible evidence that life would ever get any better.

Yet I had faith. The faith of my father. A faith that I knew was real.

I took these verses and more and tied them around my heart. I would not give up. God could come down at any moment and change things if He wanted to. I didn't know how or when, but I knew He could.

And I trusted He would.

20

THE NEEDLE AND THE DAMAGE DONE

I was a dead man walking.

I couldn't stop, couldn't even slow down, while every single inch of my skin and my soul wanted to collapse. The work I was doing meant everything and nothing, just like the rest of the world. A world I could no longer see, a place I no longer recognized. I had created my own isolated little corner where I stuck a needle in my arm and stoked a burning fire and kept every other living thing at arm's length.

I was dying—there was no doubt about that.

Not long before the last week of a lengthy and perilous journey, I literally almost died.

I couldn't get enough, yet I wanted more. I forced more and more drugs into my system, feeding the flames with something that would never fulfill and would always,

always, always burn out. But I kept feeding, hungry, my mind so gone and my will so absent.

I remember the moment I found myself crawling over my bedroom floor knowing there was no one in the house to cry to and realizing God above wasn't about to help a stupid fool like me. My latest cocktail of choice had been a batch of cocaine and meth. Sounds so glamorous, so rebellious, so raw and real. But the only glamorous thing was the way the stars lit up all around my hazy head, and the only rebellious thing was the way I was pounding on my chest trying to get my heart going again. I couldn't breathe and sweat covered my forehead and I knew I was having a heart attack. I cursed and choked and thought, *I'm dying right on the floor right by my bed and right next to the hollowed-out post where I hide all my drugs.*

The drugs and needles were still on the ground surrounding me. I could only make it to the armchair in the corner of the room. I pulled myself up and tried to keep breathing.

I could hear a line from a favorite Pink Floyd song stirring in the back of my head.

"Come on you stranger, you legend, you martyr, and shine!"

The voices of my friends and my allies and my fellow soldiers on this long, hard-fought battle were singing to me. But I wasn't shining. I was dying.

I got caught in the cross fire and everything was blowing out into the stars into the fading light of the midday.

I breathed. Again. And again.

God, for some reason, had spared my life.

You'd think I'd stop, wouldn't you? But I still needed to shine like the crazy diamond that I was.

What a fool.

Oh, but this fool had some really awesome ideas when he was on meth.

In the midst of my addiction, the haze omnipresent but in my mind the coast and the horizon crystal clear, I would work all hours of the day and keep lists of ideas only a man as talented and brilliant as I was could come up with. These lists were everywhere.

I would build and trademark the wooden woodpecker house.

I would create a table with a built-in bowl where you could put your salad dressing or your salsa.

I thought every family should have a six-story life-size playhouse on their back lawn. Custom-built by M&M and handcrafted by the man, the myth, the legend Mac Owen.

How about doors that opened up and down instead of sideways?

How about bird feeders with built-in speakers?

How about a bookshelf that resembled a smiley face after all the books were placed inside it?

Oh, the ideas were endless, and they were epic. At least in my mind.

I'd think about them and start work on them, but they never really saw light of day. Because most were ridiculous. But I was working and thinking and dreaming and continuing to be as high as a kite.

I needed someone to either cut the cord or pull me back down to earth.

That final long, lost week of my addiction, I didn't sleep for a week straight. A whole week. Yet the drugs were beginning to not work. My body was shutting down and I was starting to miss whenever I shot up. The meth intended to go in my vein was pooling underneath the skin, creating a painful swelling right around the blood vessel.

My veins were literally waving the white flag. They were like troops on a death march, literally collapsing.

Whenever I injected, I'd feel a burning sensation. The high didn't last as long or wasn't as strong. I was in pain and tired, but I needed to keep going. The few times I saw Mary and the girls, I was a walking zombie, busy and distracted. There in body, but not in mind or spirit.

I had been climbing this mountain for so long, and now I was in the death zone without any oxygen to aid my ascent. I had reached the summit, but it was cloudy and dark and cold and I knew I was going to die.

God needed to intervene, but I was too far gone even to ask Him for help.

Thankfully someone else was praying for me. And had been for a very long time.

21

ANGEL

IT seemed like our youngest child was born ready to go. That's the way Callie has been from the moment I gave birth to her.

I wasn't scared but rather was looking forward to her arrival. I thought of myself as a pro at this point. I was at home when my water broke. I wasn't sure I was in labor, so Mac took me to the doctor. By the time we walked into the office, my jeans were wet from top to bottom, and I waddled in like a duck. After I signed in and sat down in a chair, the nurse called me to the back. When I stood up, the whole chair was drenched. I busted out in tears because I was so embarrassed.

"I guess I'm in labor," I said.

The nurse was apologetic and whisked me to a room. She told me the doctor would check just to make sure. Since it was the day before Thanksgiving, my regular OB doctor wasn't there. One of his associates soon arrived and we talked casually as if it were a routine checkup. But after examining me, he suddenly became a lot more serious.

"We have to get you to the hospital immediately," he said. "You're already five centimeters dilated."

We were so excited and called all the family to get there as quickly as possible. Yet I still believed we had plenty of time before the baby would come. Both our son's labor and Cherry's labor had lasted ten to twelve hours, so I naturally assumed Callie would be the same. But she didn't have the patience for a twelve-hour delivery. She wanted to get out and meet us all and get going.

She didn't even have the patience to wait on my doctor. Dr. Hall was called and rushed to be there for the delivery, but by the time he showed up to the hospital, wearing a T-shirt and blue jeans, Callie had already arrived.

Just like her big sister's, Callie's birth was an amazing miracle. Mac and I were ecstatic. Once again here was a gift that I felt we didn't deserve, but God gave to us anyway. Callie was wide-eyed and looking around at her new surroundings. She had a mound of curly hair just like Cherry, along with rosy cheeks and a plump little body. She found her fist and started sucking on it immediately. When the family saw her in the nursery, she was doing the same thing—looking out at them while sucking her fist. Full of energy and ready to meet the new world—that was our beautiful Callie.

It was a Sunday morning, February 21, 1988, when God chose to answer my prayers. I didn't know the morning would be any different from the others. I was busy getting the girls ready for church while Mac actually slept in our bed, something he didn't seem to do much those days. I'd given up on trying to get him to go to church. I didn't expect our lives to suddenly change, but God had other plans.

So did four-year-old Callie.

Picture a little girl in a pink dress and pigtails standing by the king-size bed watching her father sleeping. This wasn't unusual, but as I noticed Callie staring at Mac, I saw a different look on her face. It was frustration.

"How come Daddy doesn't do anything with us anymore?"

The world suddenly shut off and went silent for a moment.

Of course your father does things with you—he's just busy and he works long and hard and it's just a season we're in.

I was already trying to reason and rationalize in my mind, the same way I'd been doing for years. Yet I knew Callie's question was legitimate. I knew we'd been in this season for a very long time.

"How come he doesn't go to church with us?" Callie asked.

"Sweetie, he's been working really hard," I told her as I tried to get her out of our bedroom. "You just need to leave him alone and let him get some sleep."

I knew what Mac was like when he was in one of those moods. I didn't want to be around him. I didn't want Cherry and Callie to be around him, either.

Callie stood her ground. Stubborn and defiant, just like her father. "If he ain't going to church, I ain't going."

The sassy little thing, hands on her sides, her four-year-old self so determined, wouldn't leave the bedroom. I had to order her out and get us to church. These girls were my responsibility and had been for a long time. I needed to take care of them. I needed to answer their questions, since their father was never around to hear them.

We soon left for church, where the sermon was on confession. I put on a good face and a sweet smile and acted like everything was perfect in my life. Yet I couldn't hold back the tears when we sang the last song of the day, "It Is Well with My Soul."

I sang the words, trying to find peace and security in them. I sang them, but they came out weak and frail, just like my battered spirit.

I thought of the man I'd left in our bed, a man I no longer knew, a shadow of the man I'd married. It wasn't well with his soul, and because of that, it wasn't well with mine, either. It wasn't well with our daughters. It wasn't well with anybody.

I shook as I fought back the tears in that pew. I stood there singing, all alone, wondering when God would finally—*finally*—make things truly well with my soul.

But God was already at work on that front. Back home, God was finally waking Mac up and breaking down his stubborn, strong-willed spirit.

22

ROLL AWAY THE STONE

MAYBE angels fought over this moment happening right now. Maybe it was always meant to be. This twenty-nine-year-old man resting in his bed hearing the engine of the car start and thinking of his three little ladies slipping away. Leaving him alone.

Maybe God orchestrated all of this to come to a head at this very moment. I didn't know. I was tired. No. I wasn't just tired. I was empty. I was the lake behind our house, drained and dried up and filthy. I needed to be cleansed. I needed those Living Waters to come rushing and gushing over my soul.

I needed help.

I needed forgiveness.

I needed God to hear me.

My body shook, and I knew this was the moment.

Everything I had done—every choice I had made and every habit I had formed—every single thing had brought me to this awful, aching moment.

I could see my heart, broken into a hundred porcelain pieces on the floor.

I could see my soul, scarred over and tough and impenetrable.

Please, God, help me.

I needed more than help. I needed rescuing. I needed deliverance.

I was killing everything and everyone around me. Mary. Cherry. Callie. My family and my friends.

Ultimately, I was running away from God, who had been chasing me my entire life.

He had been there all along. Helping me. Leading me to safer waters. Bringing me to those I needed to be with. He brought me to Louisiana. He brought me to Mary. He brought me here to this place, but now all I could do was rest on my knees asking for help. Asking for forgiveness. Asking for mercy.

I didn't know what to do.

I didn't know where to go.

There was too much in me to change. I couldn't be someone else. I was Mac Owen. Good ole Mac Owen, the life of the party. The guy who got it done. You asked for something, and by God I made it happen. All I wanted was some relief and some fun and some escape.

Yet after trying so hard and running so fast and furious through this fog, I finally had a moment of clarity.

Callie's words had ripped through me like a knife. I was gutted and could feel everything coming out.

God, can You take this away?

It was a nice thought, but I didn't know. I didn't know if things *could* be any different. I couldn't change, could I? After everything that had happened, I was still running away. Doing it my way. Doing everything I wanted and trying to escape. Wanting to keep the laughter and the high alive.

I kept trying to float away, but I was there on the floor, a broken man all alone and about to lose everything.

God, help me.

Callie's words were haunting me.

Suddenly I saw the whole world differently.

Suddenly I knew what I needed to do.

If I didn't get out of this room and change things, I was going to lose everything. Those women and this life and every part of me.

I took a deep breath. I wasn't sure I could do it.

You don't need to start today, one voice said.

You're just tired you need a little pick-me-up, another voice whispered.

But Callie's words were louder. More real. The other voices died that day.

I stood up and went to do something I should have done a long time ago.

But it wasn't just me moving here. God was helping me. Every single step of the way.

23

LANDSLIDE

I arrived home with the girls, uncertain what we'd find. The house was silent. As the girls played, I went to our bedroom. That's where I saw him, sitting in the recliner, seemingly unable to move. The moment I saw him, I knew something was different. He glanced at me in a way that shook me a lot, like the first time I saw that boy walking past me in the hallway.

Those defiant, devil-may-care eyes were gone. In their place were tears. His eyes were swollen and red. I'd never seen Mac cry, ever, in our whole marriage. Never once, not about the son we gave up, not about anything.

I knew something was wrong with him—something had been wrong with him for a very long time—yet I didn't know what to say.

Then I noticed that he had a big old legal-size yellow pad in his hands. The page was full.

Those glassy, worn-out eyes looked at me as he handed the pad to me. I saw that at the top it said *Dear Mary.*

One part of me was afraid to read this. Was he finally done with our family? Had the madness finally taken control of every last bit of him?

Yet I took this letter to me with an assurance that only God could have given me. I sat down on the floor beside Mac as I read.

Dear Mary,

I don't know how else to tell you what I'm feeling, so I'm gonna write it down. I've been doing crystal meth. I want to quit. I don't know how to do it. I just know it hurts you guys and I don't want to do it anymore.

I just spent the last hour burning everything I could in the big trash barrel outside. I burned it all—my drugs and needles and scales—everything. They're all gone.

I know I've been gone for a long time, Mary. I want to come home. I want to be the man you want me to be—to be the man you need me to be. I want to be a godly man. For you and for our girls.

I've asked God for forgiveness and for help. I'm asking you to forgive me as well. I don't know what else to do or where to go, but I want us to figure it out. I just know I have to stop or I'm going to die.

I love you, Mary. I love Cherry and Callie. I don't want to hurt y'all anymore. I want to be a family. A real family. I want to start over again.

I want to do the right thing and I want to start today.

Mac

I wiped the tears off my face and looked at Mac. He was no longer a stranger. Suddenly I understood everything. Every mood swing and disappearance, every argument over money, everything.

A fresh breeze of air blew through me. It was hope, and it was precious.

I didn't hug Mac and kiss him and tell him everything was going to be okay, because I didn't know if it would. But I finally knew what was happening.

I'd been so focused on trying to make our home look normal for our girls and the church that I was in total denial that my husband might be an addict. I thought there might be a demon living in him. I thought he had lost his mind. So when he told me all he was doing, I actually felt relief. Mac wasn't losing his mind, and neither was I. We were just in the center of a battle being waged right there.

I could tell in his eyes that he was tired of the lies and truly wanted to change. At the same time, I wasn't going to say, "Okay, let's just start over." I knew that we needed help. I was worn out from all the secrets. I didn't care what anybody else thought anymore. I just prayed that somebody would help us out of this hellhole. And Mac felt the same way.

I can do this. I can work with this. We *can figure this thing out.*

The *we* included God. He would be the one who needed to help and guide us.

Mac had always been the take-charge guy, the one springing into action. I was the one who allowed him to take care of me and make the decisions. I depended on him and tried to make things better. But everything was different now.

I was still holding the letter in my hands. "We need to call Ray," I said to Mac. "Would you talk to him?"

Ray Melton was the minister at our church, and he had always liked Mac for some reason—maybe because he was a recovering alcoholic himself. He'd come to the shop and ask Mac to build things for him. Mac thought of him as just an old country guy who was cool. As Mac said, Ray wasn't "high church."

Mac nodded and said one simple word in reply.

One simple and amazing word.

"Yeah."

24

ABOUT TO BEGIN

IT was time.

My heart beat as I sat in the pew, finally ready to give in. Finally ready to give over every single thing I had left. I could give my possessions to the poor and could make pieces of furniture for those in need. But I was about to give up my pride, and I had a whole warehouse full of it.

That afternoon, after Mary's father picked up the girls and left the two of us alone, Ray came by our house to help us out. He looked me in the eyes and said, "Hey, we can beat this thing."

We all agreed that it would be best for Mary and me to go to the evening church service. There was an altar call waiting that had my name written all over it.

"Now you don't have to tell everybody at church," Ray said. "But if you do, you may actually help somebody else who's struggling with the same thing."

"I gotta tell them all," I agreed. "'Cause if I don't, I'll go back and use again."

This was a lot for Mary to take in, but she wasn't leaving my side. She seemed to have a newfound determination in her spirit. Maybe because she was finally hearing the truth.

After we'd talked with Ray for a couple of hours, Mary called her dad to let him know what was happening and that we would be responding to the altar call. Mary's father answered just like always. With strength and grace. "Mac has a little problem, and we will deal with it as a family."

So there we were in the front pew at the end of the Sunday evening service, and when the pastor gave the altar call, Mary and I stood up.

Hey, that's good ole Mac; what's going on?

My body shook, and I knew there was no turning around.

I want to change. I want to begin again. I want help.

The church members were singing a song, "Just As I Am" or something like that. I felt more safe in this place than I'd ever felt in my entire life.

God, show me what You want me to do.

A hardened heart that had been broken was finally moldable again.

I was asking for help and telling everybody I knew that I needed to change.

I was ready to do anything—anything—somebody told me.

So there in front of a congregation of four hundred church members, a new chapter began. I didn't know what God had planned, and really, I just wanted to get through these next few moments and make it to tomorrow. I still couldn't look down the road.

I thought of the floating ashes of the fire in that fifty-five-gallon trash barrel behind our house; they represented my life up to that point. Twenty-nine years of what? For what? As those ashes drifted through the air, I had prayed that things could be different. That God would take these ashes and do something good. For His sake and glory.

25

SILVER SPRINGS

THERE *can be a happy ending here.*

I kept thinking that. Believing it. Even as we stood in front of the congregation and the minister read the letter he'd asked Mac to write. It was Mac's second honest letter of the day, where he told everybody publicly that he was addicted to drugs and needed help and had nowhere else to go but to our church family. Ray prayed over us and said we were courageous to come forward and as a congregation they would stand with us.

Stand with us and never let us go.

As Ray prayed for us, people started coming down to the front. Soon almost all of those four hundred people were there in the front of the church, surrounding us and making it clear we weren't alone. They cried with us and hugged us. And over and over again, we heard the same thing: "We don't know what to do with you—you are our first drug addict."

But even louder than that, we heard this: "We want you to keep coming back. We don't know how to help, but we will find out."

We were there for an hour after the church service. It was an incredible time of love poured out on us.

During that time a church member named Nancy, who was a nurse, came up to me and said she knew of a facility that we might want to investigate. When we got home and I mentioned this to Mac, he was skeptical.

"I don't need that," he said. "I'm not crazy. Rehab's for crazy people."

I didn't tell Mac that I'd been living with a crazy person for the last few years.

"I said I'd turn my life around, and that's all I got to do," he said.

I knew that Mac wanted to turn his life around and fully intended to do everything he could to make that happen. But as strong as Mac might be, I knew he couldn't do it alone. Even if we had each other and the support of our church and the help of God on our side, we needed professional help, and I told Mac that.

"If that's what you want me to do, I'll go do it," he said. "But I'm just telling you, the doctors aren't going to want me to stay."

We were emotionally drained and went straight to bed holding each other and wondering what the future would look like. We felt a sense of relief that we weren't holding that particular secret anymore. One day at a time was all we could think of. One step at a time, one moment at a time was how we were going to live our lives.

When we visited the facility the next day, Mac was surprised to hear they did indeed want him to stay. He reluctantly conceded, telling the counselors he needed to go back home and get his stuff.

"Your stuff's in the trunk," I told him.

Mac hadn't seen me pack his suitcase and put it in the car. I knew there was no way he was coming back home.

I tried to assure him that this was the right thing to do, that everything was going to work out fine. "Mac, this is the beginning of our new life. I don't want to go back down that road again. So whatever it takes for us to get there, let's do it."

I was not talking in the singular. Not anymore. *We* were in this thing now. We were still stuck out in the middle of that dark and murky lake with the storm clouds above us, but we'd finally climbed back into the boat. Together.

Mac was moldable at that point and ready to do anything anybody said.

If you knew Mac then, you'd realize how truly miraculous this was.

There can be a happy ending here.

Those Bible verses I'd been praying daily finally made sense.

I had asked God repeatedly to change Mac's life.

Every single word I prayed was heard.

Every single moment I cried out in anguish was watched.

Every single hurt I held was known.

God loved Mac and me and Cherry and Callie. He loved the boy we'd given up.

I had waited and waited and waited a little longer. God knew when it was time.

For Mac and me, it was time.

We had a lake full of hurts, habits, and hang-ups that we were about to start wading through, but we were ready.

We were ready.

PART TWO

MORE AND MORE LIKE HIM

26

TURN THE PAGE

YOU know the worst thing you could ever hear come out of a redneck's mouth?

"Watch this."

It's the worst because he's probably fixing to die.

But you know what I love? I love it when *God* says, "Watch this."

Because He's fixing to do something that's totally amazing.

I believe God finally told Satan enough. I think He finally said to watch this and watch out.

Mary and I were in His hands, and He had good things planned.

Upon arrival in rehab, I was in a group of twenty people. On the first day the doctors said to us: "Only one out of twenty of you is going to stay sober. Those are the statistics."

Without hesitation, I looked at the whole group and told them, "I'm the one."

I could see the contempt in their eyes. One guy looked at me in disbelief and told me that was kind of arrogant.

"Oh no, you don't get it," I said. "I've got to be the one. If I don't, I die. I have to do whatever it takes."

Maybe the doctors had heard this kind of talk before, this kind of bravado and belief. But I knew myself and knew there wasn't another option. I planned on tackling this thing the only way I knew how.

So let me back up for a moment and tell you about the totem pole.

Cherry once came home from school with a project for us to do. "Dad, I have to make a totem pole for a class project."

I was like "No problem. Let's go."

"Where are we going?"

"To get the stuff to make a totem pole," I told her.

We went out to the shop to get the chain saw. Then we walked down to the swamp to cut down a tree and take all its bark off. I got Cherry working on it right away, with little Callie helping out. We made a totem pole almost six feet tall, with heads carved in it, beaks, the wings up top, and painted colors all the way down to the stand. It was the coolest totem pole ever.

When Cherry and I were finished, I stood there with her looking at it proudly.

"*Now* we got us a totem pole."

The next day I followed my daughter into her classroom carrying the totem pole on my shoulders. Meanwhile, other kids were holding their totem poles in their hands. Most were made out of either toilet paper rolls or pencils or construction paper. Nobody told me we were supposed to make *faux* totem poles!

Cherry's teacher stood there with an open mouth. "I've never seen a totem pole quite like that," she said. At the end of the day, she asked if the class could keep it.

I had been brought up with the motto "If a job is worth doing, then do it right or don't do it at all." They had asked for a totem pole, and Cherry and I built one. We gave it our all, not cutting any corners, not making any quick fixes or shortcuts. It took us a lot longer, but the totem pole we built lasted. It made an impression on the others who saw it. And it stayed in that classroom for years.

My recovery would end up resembling that totem pole.

That first week was tough. When Mary left me there, the huge metal doors slammed shut and I was locked in, looking out the thin panes of glass. I heard each of her steps as her heels clicked on the tile floor. Tears rolled down my cheeks as I wondered, *Will she really come back?*

The doctors were amazed that I was still alive. They said the amount of meth I was doing should have killed me. They had to medically detox me, because they said if I quit cold turkey, it would be like severe trauma, and I could have a heart attack or a stroke from my body going into shock. That first week they gave me lithium to calm my body.

Instead of sleeping the normal sixteen hours a week I was accustomed to, I slept for sixteen hours a day. In those nineteen days in rehab I gained thirty pounds. I couldn't eat enough. My clothes suddenly didn't fit because I was the human disposal.

I kept praying to God to take this addiction away from me. I prayed from the bottom of my soul, from a place I didn't even know existed. The tears had started and they weren't going away. It was like I'd finally realized that's what those things were there for.

I get it, God. I'm a mess. I need You. I'm broken and need fixing.

Seven days of detoxing weren't going to fix so many years of poor choices and habits. But they were a start.

They were a start. And I literally and truly was taking it a day at a time.

Two years into my recovery, I learned that I was the only one out of those twenty in the room that day who was still sober and hadn't relapsed.

It wasn't because the road was smooth sailing.

It's because God is good and I continually surrounded myself with God's people.

And, for some reason, He allowed me to be the one.

27

HE IS RISEN

GOD, *help me. Give me strength today. Let Your face shine down on me today.*

This is what I prayed before leaving our house. It had been seven days. Seven long and silent days since I said good-bye to Mac as he went off to rehab. They wouldn't let him talk to anyone, including me, while he was detoxing for a week. I finally received a call from the hospital saying I could visit, and I was nervous.

As I drove across the Cheniere Dam that morning, the sun reflected off the lake. I thought of the last image of Mac before going into rehab. His sweet smile just before those huge metal doors closed. Considering the medical staff's warning about detoxing from meth, I wasn't sure what to expect.

Was the same Mac I'd said good-bye to going to greet me, or would it be an entirely new person? Would he still have his sense of humor? That mischievous grin? That wide-eyed *let's-do-this-thing* attitude about everything?

I felt a shiver of fear go through my body.

I glanced out over the blue water and suddenly heard a voice as if it were in the passenger seat beside me.

YOU HAVE A STORY TO TELL.

The voice was clear, but the message made no sense. This wasn't a story we were going to tell people. Mac was going to get better and we were going to move on with our lives. God knew our pain and that was fine, but nobody else needed to be reminded what we were going through. Mac had messed up and he was getting help. This was something that would stay between Mac and me.

YOU ARE GOING TO TELL YOUR STORY
TO MANY PEOPLE.

For a moment my knees felt weak and I could barely push on the gas. I was tired and confused and scared.

We can't let other people know all this; they won't understand. They will look down on us and judge us. I don't want our girls living that kind of life.

YOU ARE GOING TO TELL YOUR STORY
TO MANY PEOPLE.

The words kept playing over in my head. And each time they did, I felt something strange. Not the tremble of worry, but rather that light touch of peace.

I looked up at the heavens and wondered what God had planned for Mac and me. This thing had just happened. We had barely begun to change, to get help, to get Mac better. So the thought of telling others, of telling our story to "many people," seemed ludicrous. Yet it also felt right.

I had asked for God's help this morning, and this was His answer. I knew then and I know now God was speaking to me in a very clear voice that day.

Yet at the time I quickly tried to forget about this encounter. I wasn't ready to tell the world about what was happening. I wanted to just sweep it under the rug. The man I had married wanted to make it through each day. His story and journey were just starting.

Little did I realize another journey was about to begin as well. It involved the son we had given up twelve and a half years before.

A son named Heath.

28

TEARS IN HEAVEN

I didn't realize a man could harbor such deep and endless hurt inside his heart. As my mind and my body began to adjust to their new clean lives, I experienced emotions I had never felt my entire life. My body wasn't just tired—my soul was tired. I desperately knelt before the cross day after day—hour after hour—and asked Jesus for mercy. For grace. For hope.

I felt buried under this avalanche I'd created and allowed to smother me. Little by little, I was digging out.

But a week into recovery, I still felt dark and breathless and unsure where to go.

I felt alone and abandoned. I felt like my life up to this point had been pointless and painful. What was I supposed to do now? Where was I supposed to go?

I kept Mary and Cherry and Callie and the son we would never know at the front of my mind. But the doubts and the whispers of despair threatened me.

As strong as I was and knew I could be, I was also weak and powerless.

You'll never be able to be whole.

So they whispered.

God is not going to bless you. Look at you, you pathetic loser.

So they mocked.

Every friend and family member is going to abandon and leave you, just you wait.

So they lied.

Then I saw Mary, and she reminded me I wasn't alone. And the next day I received a gift from our church. Actually, seven hundred gifts.

The church that said they didn't quite know what to do with me—their first drug addict—had passed out love-o-grams at the worship service the following Sunday. So the next day I received a bulging legal-size manila envelope full of notes and cards.

I wasn't sure what to think or feel as I read them. Card after card said the same thing. I was dear and I wasn't forgotten. People were praying for me. People were wishing me the best. Children who didn't even understand what I was dealing with were telling me to get better. Me—Mac, the guy using needles and shooting up with meth, the guy who'd basically abandoned his family for the last two years—everybody was wishing me well and hoping I'd get better.

They haven't forgotten.

Some of the notes were short and sweet. Some were long and filled me with surprise and awe. Every single one gave me hope. Hope and assurance that I wasn't alone, that God wasn't judging me, that I wasn't going to be defined by the mistakes I'd spent twenty-nine years making.

God's got a plan for you, someone wrote.

Rely on Jesus and He'll get you through this, someone else wrote.

We love you, they all said, over and over and over again.

Even though Mary had gone home and I was in my room by myself, I no longer felt alone. I felt the need and the craving to use—sure. I would have those cravings for another five years. But on this day, a week into recovery, I felt loved. I felt valued. I felt hope.

This was God saying, *I still love you, Mac. I always have, from the moment you took in your first breath and gave out your first cry. I loved you then and I love you now.*

There were more tears. Boy, were there more tears. For years to come.

And like those letters and cards and notes, every single tear was a reminder of God's limitless and bottomless and endless love.

It was also a sign:

There's no turning back, Mac. Not now. You can do this.

You can do this.

29

DON'T STOP

A new chapter in a new journey was about to begin. It had nothing to do with Mac's recovery, however.

Nothing and everything.

A month after the miracle of Mac finally waking up and asking for help in his life, another miracle happened.

I still find it unbelievable that God allowed this to happen at just that time. I think He was waiting patiently on Mac to come to Him. I feel like once that happened, God said, "Because you are yielding to Me, here is a gift. I am going to give you the desire of your heart."

And so He did, in the most miraculous way.

It wasn't as though I'd ever forgotten about the son we gave up. I carried his memory around with me on a daily basis. I mourned the son we had never met while continuing to pray for his well-being. I hoped that one day Mac and I might be able to meet him. Just to see how he was doing. Just to look him in the eyes.

Just once.

In June 1980 I had called the lawyer who took care of the adoption, asking to know anything about our son. Mainly, I wanted to know if he was in a loving home. The lawyer told me his name: Heath.

Heath. Sweet Heath.

Not long after that, a picture came. Heath's parents had given the lawyer a wallet-size picture of him in kindergarten. I cried and prayed over that little picture until it was worn out.

Every few months after this, I would call the lawyer wanting to know more. But he would just assure me Heath was in a loving family and we couldn't know more.

It was 1984 when the lawyer said we could write a letter to Heath's parents and he would give it to them. We wrote a letter and included our phone number in it.

October 8, 1984

Mrs. Arthur,

I've been wanting to write you for a long time and finally decided to do it. I am Heath's birth mother. We are Christians, and I would never do anything to hurt y'all or Heath in any way, so please don't worry that I ever would. I want him to have a normal, uncomplicated childhood.

Our situation is unique in that his father, Mac, and I got married a year and a half after his birth. Because of my age then (Mac is a year younger than me and was still in high school), and because my mother was extremely sick (she never even knew I was pregnant), and a number of other things, I decided this was best for Heath. I wanted him to have a normal childhood with a mom and dad. I thank God every day for y'all loving him and taking him into your lives nine years ago.

Heath has two sisters, Cherry—four years old and Callie—ten months old.

I hope when Heath gets older that maybe we could all be friends. Y'all are his parents, and I would never want to change that. From what I've heard, most adopted children want to meet their birth parents out of curiosity when they are grown. I hope that will be the case with Heath. I want him to know one day that we love him and did then when he was born. (I think that would help an adopted child's self-esteem, to know he wasn't given up because he wasn't loved.)

It would mean so much to me if you would send a picture of him. I've always wondered if he favors his sisters.

There is so much I would like to tell you about us and what happened back then if you want to know. May the Lord bless you.

Sincerely,

Mary Owen

It was a Sunday morning while we were getting ready for church when the Arthurs called us. They were defensive at first and very wary of these people interested in the child they'd given up, but after a long heartfelt conversation they understood where we were coming from. For a few months after that we wrote back and forth until the letters suddenly stopped on their end. (Later we learned that they had been advised by friends not to communicate with us for fear of what we might be wanting to do.)

Right around this period of time, I began to write to Heath in a journal. I thought Mac and I would never meet him in person. This was back in the days before the Internet, and finding someone and reaching out to them was a lot more difficult to do. If we died, I wanted to make sure Heath would learn that we loved him and thought of him on his birthday and holidays (and all the other days of the year, for that matter). I desperately wanted him to know his two sisters, especially when I realized he was an only child.

Writing in a journal was incredibly cathartic for me. In the beginning, it was more for my own sanity and healing. I wasn't writing for Heath but for myself, trying to make peace with God in my heart for what we had done.

I hoped and dreamed that one day we might be able to meet Heath. But I never imagined what the future held. I couldn't dream that big.

I've learned God makes the unimaginable happen.

"Mary, you'll never believe where I am."

It was two in the morning when the phone woke us up. I was surprised to find my sister-in-law Chrys on the other line. Whispering.

"Chrys? What's wrong? Where are you?"

"I'm in Heath's bed!"

I was still half-asleep, but I heard what she said. All I could think was that she was talking about a family at our church with the last name of Heath.

"What are you doing in Mr. Heath's bed?"

"No, no—Heath, your son!"

Johnny and Chrys were still the only people other than my father who knew about the son we'd given up. They'd faithfully kept our secret, and they knew about my correspondence with Heath's parents.

In spring of 1988, a month after Mac had gone into rehab, our church youth group attended a youth rally five hours away in Lafayette, Louisiana. Chrys happened to be one of the chaperones on that trip. So many kids came that not everybody could fit in the houses around the host church, so the organizers reached out to other churches asking families to host some of the kids. One family that happened to answer the call lived over half an hour away and attended a church in Lafayette.

Their last name was Arthur.

So out of all these thousands of kids and chaperones, who was assigned to the Arthurs? They didn't even live close to the rally site and had no plans to help with the housing until they got a phone call.

Chrys, her daughter Korie, and Korie's friend all climbed into the car of the really nice couple who came to pick them up. On the ride to their house, Chrys asked if they had any children.

"We have a son," the woman said. "He's attending the rally."

"Oh, really? What's his name?"

Chrys knew their last name was Arthur, but she hadn't made the connection. It was a common name and a very big state.

"Heath."

There's no way this can be Mac and Mary's Heath. That's crazy.

She still didn't believe it—I mean, come on, what were the odds?—so Chrys asked them how old their son was.

"Twelve."

It took everything in Chrys not to have a heart attack in the backseat of that car. It was too impossible. Too crazy even to think about.

Could these really be parents of their son, their Heath?

Chrys composed herself and tried to keep her pulse from racing and her voice from overreacting. She continued to talk with the Arthurs, her heart still in disbelief, her mind searching for a way to know for sure. Eventually she managed to ask another question about Heath.

"So when's his birthday?"

"August 17," Mrs. Arthur said.

Suddenly Chrys's disbelief turned to fear. How could they help but be suspicious if they learned the truth. Chrys remembered my saying that the Arthurs had told us if we ever tried to find out where they were, they'd move away to somewhere we'd never find them.

They'll never believe I just happened to get in their car. I can barely believe it myself.

So the rest of the evening Chrys didn't say a word about Mac or me or knowing who Heath was. She waited until everybody had gone to bed and the house was quiet; then she called me collect in the middle of the night so it wouldn't show up on their phone bill.

Her heart was still racing as she tried desperately to be quiet and calm. She told me she had seen pictures of Heath all over the house—baby pictures even! I'd never seen any baby pictures of Heath. We had only that one wrinkled and faded kindergarten picture the lawyer had sent.

"They love Heath and take good care of him."

These were the words I'd wanted to hear—that I'd *needed* to hear—for so long. Outside of Mac telling me he was going to change, I couldn't imagine anything that could bring more hope and light to my heart.

I held the phone in my hand but was now jumping up and down on the bed, relaying to Mac what was going on and why I was suddenly acting like a possessed woman.

"Mac, you're not gonna believe this!" I was screaming at him while bouncing around.

All this time—all these years...

You couldn't make this sort of thing up. A fiction writer would've changed the story line because it was too unbelievable. Too coincidental. Too unlikely.

But isn't that the way God works best? When He finally says, *Let me show you what can happen if I want it to.*

The Arthurs, as it turned out, couldn't have children. They had tried for ten years to adopt, but it had never happened for them. For a while they thought of giving up. Then suddenly, out of the blue, there came a lawyer with a baby, looking for a Christian family. It turns out they only had a couple of days to even prepare.

By the time I got off the phone with my sister-in-law, both Mac and I were sitting there on the bed, bug-eyed in true shock. A joyous disbelief. We were hugging each other and laughing and crying.

Only one month earlier, in this same bedroom, Mac had looked at his life and seen the absolute wreckage of it. He had only seen dark clouds and menacing shadows. Hope was gone, and all he could do was cry out.

But now...now God was telling us, *It's going to be okay. And oh yeah, by the way, your son is okay too.*

That whole weekend Chrys acted nonchalant, though I had told her to try to take a picture of Heath. The only picture she got—one we still have—was of the back of Heath's head at the youth rally. She told me that Heath got up to say a prayer at the rally and when he went to sit back down, she took a picture.

The secret was so much to carry around with her that Chrys had to tell her daughter. Korie was fourteen at the time and surely could tell her mother was acting a bit strange.

"Korie, I'm fixing to tell you something," Chrys told her in private. "You're really too young to hear all this, but I can't keep this to myself. It's just too huge. I've got to tell somebody."

So Chrys told Korie about the baby we gave away and who had been adopted by the Arthurs. That baby was their son, Heath.

"Korie, this is a secret we have to keep. And we might even have to take it to the grave."

It was such a relief—such a miracle—to know Heath was in a loving family and that God was blessing him. My prayers and my hopes had been answered.

Could I dare pray and hope for more?

30

WHAT'S YOUR NAME?

RECOVERY was a new world for me. The night Mary and I went to the front of the church to tell them what was happening with me, I remember a little lady telling me that I needed to go to AA.

I nodded at her and said, "That's like the car club, right?"

She shook her head. "No, that's *triple* A. You need double A."

I was ready to do whatever anybody suggested. So early on, they told me I needed to go to ninety meetings in ninety days.

I made more than ninety.

Totem pole.

I was an overachiever. I went to meetings all the time. At one point even Mary was like "Okay, now I don't know if this is what I signed up for." I'd been missing in their lives for so long because of the drugs; now I was missing because of going to AA meetings and sharing things about our life. Not my life, but our lives.

Mary had wanted the white picket fence—the house and the dog in the yard and the beautiful children smiling and playing and laughing. Meanwhile I'm sharing all this ugly stuff that had been going on in our lives.

During that time our friend Barbara Kee, who was working on her doctorate in counseling, told Mary to be patient.

"It doesn't happen overnight," Barbara said. "For Mac to be the man that you've been praying for him to be—to be the man of God he needs to be—he's got to do this."

Mary realized this and stopped griping about it. In fact, she said, "If Mac's going, so am I." So we went to meetings together.

Mary's parents were so great about everything. Anytime we wanted to go to a meeting, they would come to the house and babysit. We didn't tell the girls what was happening since they were so young. While I was at the hospital in rehab for those nineteen days, Mary had told them I was sick.

When I first got in rehab, I was sleeping so much that I felt like I wasn't doing enough. The staff assured me I was doing exactly what I was supposed to be doing. I would wake up, eat, and go to AA meetings. That was my daily schedule. These meetings became a source of energy, because people from the outside who had attained sobriety would come in, and I could see the obvious joy in their lives. That motivated me to want to do better in my life.

Until the day one of the dealers I'd been buying drugs from showed up.

I knew he wasn't there for a meeting.

I went and told the nurses right away that this guy was a drug dealer; not only that, but he was still doing drugs. I was sure he was there to give somebody drugs. I was devastated and really angry. If there wasn't safety there in rehab, then what was the use?

That night, a nurse named Veronica sat beside my bed and said this to me: "Mac, there are always going to be people in your life like the man you saw tonight. You have to make a choice."

That night the clarity about my mission was unbelievable.

I need to save myself and my family. Whatever it takes. Whatever the cost.

That was when I knew without a doubt in my mind that this was going to work. That this *could* work.

God didn't totally and instantly deliver me from cravings and desires. I had to be careful with everything—from who I hung around with to the movies or television shows I watched. I couldn't watch anything that showed somebody shooting up, or even a hospital scene of sticking anything in a vein. If I did, my arms would hurt immediately and I'd cringe. Sometimes—many times—I woke up in a cold sweat, unable to breathe, afraid I had used again. Things would come up, and I'd think, *Oh yeah, it would be good to use. Oh, man.*

Sometimes I hear stories about God delivering people from those cravings so quickly. I'm usually like *Really, what was that like?* Because I still felt imprisoned and in bondage to my wants and desires. The only thing I knew was this had to work. And the only power that could make it happen was God giving me the strength and the courage.

After six months, I was already being asked to speak at events like youth rallies. Though I was still just learning this recovery thing and taking life day by day, I also wanted to help people. So I'd share whatever I could whenever I could.

Rehab and the months following were a good break for me, from everything. I would soon be amazed to find out all the people who had noticed I'd gone missing. Not just my so-called friends, either. Or the guys I bought drugs from. Others had been watching me for a while. And those same people noticed when I suddenly disappeared from the face of the earth.

After one event at which I'd shared, I was approached by a man who was visibly moved and shaken up. Something was going on with him.

"Are you Mac Owen?" he asked.

"Yeah."

"You look different," the man said in an astonished tone.

"I am different. The old Mac you knew died. This is the new Mac."

"Man, you disappeared into thin air."

Let's call him Jack Paulsen. He was on the metro drug task force and had been watching me for some time. He knew where I bought my drugs and where they were hidden.

In my house. I must have told one of my drug buddies where I had my stash, because someone had informed them. It turns out they were just about to bust me; because of all the drugs I had been buying, they assumed I was dealing. They figured nobody could be taking *that* much meth himself. But they didn't know I was an overachiever.

Jack, who ended up becoming a good friend of ours, told me I had been under surveillance for some time. They knew I was staying up all night and working in my shop. They knew the people coming to my shop to party with me. They knew where I was coming and going. Until, of course, Mary brought me to rehab, and I mysteriously vanished.

Maybe little Callie knew the authorities were onto me and decided Daddy better get his act together before he went to jail.

I joke, of course. But one person who saw all of this happening certainly helped give Callie a nudge. He also continued to help me get through each day by opening my eyes to the damage I had been doing to myself and those around me.

Even in the midst of my self-induced storms, God was watching out for me.

31

I WANT A NEW DRUG

1988 was a watershed year for my family. Not just for Mac and me and our children, but for our whole extended family. It was a year when we finally began to deal with some of those family secrets. Like the secret of Mac's addiction, which was suddenly out in the open and being dealt with. Like the secret of the child we gave up for adoption, who we now knew was blessed with a good Christian home. And like the secret of my mother's illness.

As I've mentioned, years after having battled with an unknown and undesignated disease, my mother was diagnosed a paranoid schizophrenic. Before finding any sort of known treatment, doctors prescribed all kinds of drugs just to calm her system down. For my whole youth, I remember my mother taking all this medicine that never really helped. It just dragged her down. It was as if she had these demons in her mind telling her that people were going to hurt us. That's what she worried about the most; she always thought there was somebody out to get me or my brother or sister.

My father used to encourage my mom to be around people. At times she would say she didn't want to entertain anybody, but Dad saw that she did better when she was cooking and entertaining. It took her mind off her worrying. She could pull off a full-course meal or a bridal shower in our home with ease.

But then there were times when her mental illness would spiral down to a point where she couldn't function. She was in the hospital as often as every three months, and sometimes she would be in for six weeks or more. I never worried about her being in the hospital because Dad never said anything negative about it. He would just say Mom was sick, and somehow he was able to keep our home feeling normal.

When we were young, none of us knew that anything was wrong. We all knew, for example, that our mother loved to stand in the corner and pray and read the Bible. I thought all moms did that until I became a teenager, and then all of a sudden at other people's houses I noticed something odd.

Wow, their moms don't stand in the corner praying and reading the Bible.

That's when I knew that something wasn't quite right with Mom.

I only saw my mother get aggressive once.

I was about fourteen when I heard my mother screaming one afternoon. I ran to my parents' bedroom to see my father and one of his friends on either side of her, trying to pick her up. She refused to move because she knew they were planning to take her to the hospital.

Back then, the recommendation for her illness was to receive shock treatments. The shock treatments literally were like mind erasers. My dad told me later he once saw her tongue with bloody teeth imprints where she almost bit it off because of what they were doing to her. It was torture, and she refused to be taken back.

That day as my mother refused to go, I saw the tears in my father's eyes. He didn't want to take her, but he knew there was nothing else he could do. It was the only way she would get better. Yet always, always, the treatment would wear off after several months.

My father told me about another time Mom was in the hospital. Because of the state she was in, they often had to tie her down to the bed. Somehow she had gotten loose and ended up locking the door to her room. Nobody could get inside.

Dad kept telling her, "Open the door, Jean; open the door." But she wouldn't do it. He found a bobby pin on the floor, right there by the doorknob, and ended up wiggling it around in order to open it. When he opened the door, Dad saw that my mother had climbed out the window. They were several stories up, and my mother was hanging on to the open window, ready to jump.

"Jean—Jean, what are you doing?" my father shouted.

He rushed over to her and reached out to grab her hands, pulling her back in through the opening. Dad thought he had lost her that time. Such events weren't some freak accident or momentary lapse of reason. This illness was an everyday ordeal for my mother and father. This was their lives.

Because of the heightened state of her condition and the danger she constantly put herself in, a doctor suggested to my father that she have a lobotomy. My father didn't even know what that was. The doctor told him they were doing those on patients and having good success with it.

This procedure, of course, was where they messed around with the brain. Back then they didn't know all the effects and results of operations like that. Now, of course, we know a lot more about it. Many times people who had lobotomies were never the same and turned into vegetables. But my father didn't know this and only wanted to help my mother. So he told them to go ahead with the procedure.

The night before the scheduled surgery that was going to take place two hours away in Jackson, Mississippi, my father woke up suddenly and felt he heard God speaking to him.

"Do not do that," this voice told my father. "Do not take her to get that surgery."

So the next morning he canceled the appointment.

Just as he had been with Mac and me, my father was always patient and loving to my mother. I never saw my parents fight. Nor did I ever hear him raise his voice or see him raise a hand. He always treated my mother like she was the queen of the country.

All along, we kept my mother's illness a secret from everybody. We didn't want people calling her crazy, which was what they would have done if they had known. So we kept this private, and my father took the brunt of the weight of my mother's illness.

We always hoped things would get better, but we never knew if they would.

In the same year that a four-year-old stood by her father and woke him up to reality, that little girl's mother heard about something that might wake up *her* mother from a lifetime of illness.

While watching *20/20* on television, I heard about a new drug they called "the Lazarus pill" that would literally wake people up from the dead. It was called Clozaril, and they were starting to test people in Europe on it. The amazing thing was that people who had been mentally ill were coming back to their senses—coming back to life—while using the pill.

I told my father about this, and we went to a psychiatrist and asked him about the drug. At the time, he didn't know anything about Clozaril, but after some research he told Dad the following: "Your wife is going to be the first person in Louisiana to ever be put on this. We'll try it. It will either work or not. There's no in-between."

Since my mother despised going to the hospitals, they decided to give it to her at home. The first thing that had to happen was getting her off her current medication.

So after being on all these drugs like Thorazine and Valium, she ended up going cold turkey.

It was brutal.

For several days, all my mother did was sit in the corner of the bathroom in her nightgown. I stayed there with my father to help through the process. Mom wouldn't eat, and we could barely get her to drink a little water. She was catatonic the whole time.

After a rough few days, we finally gave her this one tiny, tiny little pill before she went to bed. The next morning Dad and I came into the kitchen and there she was, totally dressed and smiling and asking what we wanted for breakfast. As if the last few days and the last few decades had not happened.

It was truly like Lazarus waking up from the dead.

I was afraid it would wear off, but it never has. There are side effects, of course, and she has to take it every night. If she doesn't, we know immediately the following morning; that paranoid look will fill her eyes again and we know something's wrong.

I find it amazing how there's just a tiny circuit somewhere in her head that doesn't connect, and by taking that one little pill, it completes that circuit.

It's sorta like the missing ingredient we all have in our broken lives. For some reason, in that year, the circuits in our family were all starting to reconnect. Jesus was picking up all our broken pieces and healing our hurts.

I had come to realize that miracles could happen, even out of the messy secrets we had kept hidden for so long.

32

WE ARE FAMILY

EARLY on in my recovery, God allowed me to come across two of the most influential people in my journey. They're also two of the most unique people I've ever met.

The first was Tommy Powell, my sponsor for the past twenty-five years.

At my first AA meeting I told the others I was an addict, and they said I couldn't be there, because this meeting was for alcoholics, not drug addicts (like there's a big difference?). So I thought, *Okay*, and cleared my throat and said, "I'm an alcoholic."

With an audible sigh of relief, they said, "Okay, you can stay."

I knew Tommy, since he attended my church. He'd been a Golden Gloves boxer in the Marines and was just plain tough. I saw him at that first AA meeting, and later on I went up and spoke to him.

"Are you like undercover AA?" I asked. "I never knew you were in the program."

Tommy looked at me. "It's an anonymous program, son. You don't just tell everybody."

I nodded and apologized. Soon after that Tommy became my sponsor.

I didn't need an average sponsor, and God knew that. I needed a totem pole sponsor. (I once told people that Tommy was an ex-Marine. Wrong move. If you're a Marine, you're a Marine for life. An "ex-Marine" means you got kicked out. I learned this the hard way.)

The first thing he did was to give me a passage of Scripture and tell me to memorize it. The next week he'd give me another.

"Man, there's no way I'll be able to do that," I said. "Too many brain cells gone."

Or so I thought.

Tommy nodded. "All right. I'm not going to be your sponsor, then."

"Whoa. No, I mean, really, honestly—I don't think I can do that."

"Yeah, you can," Tommy said. "I'll tell you how. Do not try to memorize it. Just write it down on a three-by-five card. Put the card in your pocket. Every time you think about it, you pull out the card and read it."

I thought of Mary's mother and her verses.

These three-by-five cards of Scripture have been following me half my life.

"I can do that," I said.

"Every day you write it on a new three-by-five card. Next week when you see me, you'll have it."

You know something? Tommy Powell was exactly right. I became very good at memorizing Scripture.

Turned out he was right about a lot of things.

That's what you get when you're an ex—I mean, when you're an exceptional man.

Tommy is seventy-five years old, wiry and rock hard, and still takes his role as my sponsor very seriously. Every time I see him, he'll come to me standing straight as a board (and making me stand straight as well). He looks me in the eye and says, "Mac, you know you just can't beat this, right?"

"Yes, sir, you can't beat it," I say.

Not long ago, he approached me and got inches away from my face. "Do you want to lead a good life?" Tommy asked.

"Yes, sir," I said.

"Then you need to become more obedient."

"Yes, sir," I said.

Suddenly I was doing an inventory in my head, wondering, *What have I done that he's found out about?* But I couldn't think of anything.

Tommy continued to stare at me, then finally said, "We all do. Now pass that along to the boys you sponsor." Then he walked off.

I was like *Man, you got me again.*

That's my sponsor, the one I've had for twenty-five years.

There was someone else God put into my life in those early days who has remained ever since.

This guy, Phil, was known for sharing the gospel with people. He just had a knack for it. People would come to his house to hear it. He was baptizing people. He was like a modern-day John the Baptist.

Right after getting into recovery, I thought, *This would be someone good to get to know. Someone I can learn from. Someone who can show me how to do this thing.*

So I approached him.

"Hey, I hear you like to study with people and share Jesus with them."

"Yeah, I do," Phil said.

"Well, I'd like to know how to do that. So the next time you do that, could you give me a call and I'll be right over?"

He was like "Okay, man, I'll check you later, man, no problem." Then he walked off.

About a week and a half went by, and I heard he had already had a study with somebody, witnessing and talking about Jesus. I called him up right away.

"Hey, Phil, I thought you said you were going to give me a call next time you went to study with somebody?"

He paused for a minute. "Owen, is this you?"

"Yeah, it's me. Are you, like, ashamed to call me your brother? I thought this was some kind of family deal here, you know?"

"Hey, I'll call you the next time, all right?"

Later on I'd learned that his wife, Kay, was sitting there at the time and heard his side of the phone call. Phil told her, "I think Mac's serious about this thing."

So from then on, I started to accompany Phil on these studies. There might be one or two or even three times a week when Phil would share the gospel with a non-believer. They could be anywhere at anytime. At first I shadowed him and took notes. After Phil was done sharing, I would give the person we were with my notes with all the Scriptures that he had shared written down.

We did this for almost three years.

From listening to Phil talk and from the Scripture Tommy Powell had me memorize, I started to become pretty good about witnessing to others myself.

From then on Phil and I, and Mary and Kay, took part in more and more Bible studies with people. Along the way we became good friends. Once a week we would end up having a date night with them. Mary and Kay called it a "get out of yourself night." Kay loved movies, but Phil wouldn't ever go to them unless we all went together. Phil's other love was duck hunting, something I also loved to do. We ended up hunting ducks and hunting people to share Jesus with.

Years before I met him, Phil Robertson had incorporated his love of duck hunting into a business. He called it Duck Commander. It was a small family business, run out of their home. When they got their products into Walmart, that was the beginning of it really growing.

You've probably heard of *Duck Dynasty*. That's the Phil I'm talking about, the one who mentored me in sharing the gospel. Our families would end up being connected in another cool way. Korie, the same Korie who stayed with her mother at Heath's house during a youth rally, eventually married Willie Robertson, son of Phil and Kay.

Only weeks into my recovery journey, I had already met two very important members of my Forever Family.

There were so many more to come.

33

JANIE'S GOT A GUN

"IS Mac there?"

The question almost made my heart stop. Anybody who was important in Mac's life knew exactly where he was. They knew because they were praying for him as he went through rehab. So whoever was calling me at home didn't know this part of Mac's story.

"May I ask who's calling?" I said.

"Tell him it's Anthony."

My heart started beating again. Actually, it started to race. I knew this name and knew it well. During "Family Week" in rehab, Mac had shared about Anthony. This was the guy who was the main dealer to the manufacturer, the one Mac bought from during those dark days of his addiction.

"Mac has turned his life around and is following God now," I told Anthony. "So unless you want to talk to him about Jesus, don't ever call our house again. And if I ever see your face at our front door, I have a gun and I will use it. I will kill you for what you've done to my husband."

Anthony hung up immediately.

I had never said or even thought of saying such a thing to anybody my whole life, but I was so angry for what this man had done. I felt at that moment the way I'd feel if a wolf were standing in between me and one of my babies. The strong man I'd known since sixteen was now a newborn baby in Christ, and I would do anything—any-thing—to protect him from danger. And that was danger on the other end of that telephone.

We never heard from Anthony again until eighteen years later, when he called Mac at the shop one day.

"Mac, this is Anthony; don't hang up."

"What are you doing, Anthony?" Mac asked him.

"I just wanted to let you know that I've straightened up my life and I'm a believer in Jesus Christ."

Mac was delighted to hear this and told Anthony he would love to see him. Since Anthony was now living out of state, he simply told Mac he would come see him if he was ever back in Louisiana.

Mac hasn't seen him since, but we do know one thing now.

We'll see Anthony again. If not in this lifetime, then in the next.

And I promise, Anthony. I won't be packing heat.

34

HEAVEN KNOWS

SHADOWS watch from trees and lampposts. Waiting.

Waiting to attack when you're most fragile and prone to failure.

Anthony wasn't the only person in my life I needed to watch out for. I still had a lot of friends I needed to be careful about. Most of my so-called friends suddenly disappeared after I told them I was following Jesus. These were people I'd grown up with, suddenly writing me off. That told me something about them right there.

One day shortly after getting out of rehab, I was having a rough time. The desire, as I've shared before, wasn't going away anytime soon. I still had the urge to use. On this day there were endless problems happening at the shop, the sort of silly and stupid distractions that made my job not so fun. On top of that, Mary's car broke down.

I tried fixing it, but nothing I did worked. Just like the problems at work, this was annoying.

I have enough problems to deal with. I don't need distractions at work, and I really don't need Mary's car breaking down.

Then out of the blue (and oh, can you hear the irony in my voice) up came one of my good old buddies I used to smoke with. I hadn't seen this guy since going into rehab, but while I was getting angry looking under the hood of Mary's car, lo and behold he appeared.

"What's up, Mac?"

A friend to the rescue.

After a little small talk, my buddy told me he had the answer to my problems. It was a nice big bag of dope.

"Want to go smoke?" he asked.

What are the chances of that happening? Out of the blue, on a day when I was frustrated and tired and feeling sorry for myself?

I told my friend about the changes in my life. Strangely enough, he disappeared as quickly as he had come when I shared this news with him. I went inside afterward and told Mary what had happened. The old Mac would have been smoking and then lying about smoking. The old Mac wouldn't have told Mary a word. But telling her was what I needed to do.

We agreed that temptation had come knocking at the door at a time when I was most vulnerable.

This prompted us to use a saying we heard once called HALT. Anytime we are hungry, angry, lonely, or tired, it's time to stop and do something positive and deal with the emotion.

Anytime we desired something. Or felt an overwhelming emotion. Or felt isolated and alone or exhausted. Anytime we were in any of those situations, it was time to stop. To literally *halt* and deal with what was happening.

For so many years of my life, I was used to taking the easy way out. I never once dealt with any of these things going on inside of me.

I had a lot of shadows waiting and watching to jump me at any given moment. That's why I never isolated myself. I had just crawled out of the dark well where I'd spent so many years. There was no way I was going to go back inside. No way.

35

THESE DREAMS

UNSEEN, sitting at the back of the stands, I watched him playing baseball.

I studied him talking with the other kids, running around the bases, throwing the ball, laughing and smiling.

I heard him calling out, laughing, cheering on his teammates.

Then I pictured him walking off the field after the game, scratching his thick brown hair, looking bright-eyed and handsome in his baseball uniform.

My son, my Heath, the child we'd given up on, the boy we'd given away, the life we'd given to someone else.

I want you in our lives.

So I began to follow him.

I wanted to tell him who I was and what life awaited him back home with Mac and Cherry and Callie.

Maybe Heath and I could go to the zoo, and then I could treat him to ice cream for lunch and a hamburger for dessert. Maybe there was a world fair we could go to on the way back home. I could stop by and let him see my mother and father. On the drive I'd ask him the 56,498 questions I've been saving up. Perhaps we'd get lost and end up in Canada or Mexico.

Then, somewhere between there and here, Heath would hug me and tell me it was okay, that he forgave me, that really it was no big deal. He'd tell me he still loved me and that he always would.

Back to reality, Mary Owen . . .

Some days, whenever I thought of Heath, my mind would wander and ask, "What if?" I never did go down to see him, but I thought of doing it all the time. I just wanted to see him and touch him and hear his voice.

I wanted Heath to know Mac and me.

I still didn't imagine that God would ever allow him to be in our lives. It was too big of a dream, too much of a fairy tale. But I'd still imagine. What would it be like to steal him away, just for a day?

The kindergarten picture was crumpled and already memorized. All I had was my imagination.

The same imagination that had led me to hope and believe that things could change for Mac and me.

The same imagination that dared to believe God still heard my prayers after so many years.

In my private moments, when nobody else was around, I'd still pray and ask God to answer another request from a mother about her only son.

I just didn't know if I was worthy of having those prayers answered.

August '90 (excerpts)

Dear Heath:

Mac and I decided we want to each write a journal of our thoughts and feelings about what has happened in our lives. So if something happens in our lives and we are never able to talk to you, you can read this...

We asked a counselor from our church, Barbara Kee, to talk to your parents about what Mac has been through. Mac felt it was our responsibility to tell you so maybe it would keep you from ever going down that road.

We are so grateful your parents sent us a picture of you. Mac hurts so much inside when he thinks of how he has missed raising a son. He loves you so much. He is learning through our little family how important family is and how much it means to him...

Cherry is ten and Callie is almost seven. We want to so badly tell them about you. We are praying about it very much. They are very young, but we feel we must not keep secrets anymore. I think Cherry will probably cry. She is so sensitive. Callie is so young—she will probably just say, "When we gonna see him?" I know they will be so proud to have a big brother...

Also, my dad has grieved about this all these years. He loves you too very much. My mother is on a new medicine and doing better than she has in her whole life. I know you will be such a joy to her.

When we heard about your dad baptizing you, we were so excited. We are so thankful over and over to God that you are being raised by Christian parents. That is the ultimate goal, that we all go to heaven.

We also pray that a girl is being raised to be your Christian mate and that you will have a happy and fulfilling marriage one day.

You will always be in our hearts...

Love,

Mary and Mac

36

GIVE A LITTLE BIT

MARY and I were sure there had to be lots more people in our church than just the two of us who could use some kind of twelve-step group for Christians. So we decided to go to the elders of the church and tell them of our vision and of a group we'd heard of called Overcomers Outreach.

For some reason we didn't think they'd go for it, but we figured we'd do the right thing and ask.

Then they surprised us.

"Well, that sounds pretty good. When do you all want to get started?"

I looked at Mary with a face that said, *Oh no.*

This vision didn't necessarily involve *us*. I was just starting my recovery. There was no way we could start something like this, just the two of us. So suddenly I was ready to sabotage everything.

When someone suggested that we use the little house in the parking lot of the church, I said, "Well, you know, there'll probably be smoking in there."

The elders looked around at each other.

"Didn't some of you all smoke when you got here?" one of them asked the others.

Several nodded.

"Okay, well, just make sure you clean up after yourselves," they said. "See if you can help them with that too."

"You know—there's probably going to be a lot of cussing too. Just think of what people will say."

They said, "Just think of all the things you can help them with."

Suddenly I was in complete disbelief.

They're not going to let us out of this! They're going to make us serve now.

So that's how Mary and I began as leaders in recovery. Still hung up with bad habits and deep-rooted hurts.

Sorta sounds like it should be someone's slogan, doesn't it?

So we started a chapter of Overcomers Outreach, and of course we were one of the only nonsmoking meetings in town. Back then you could smoke in AA meetings. So it didn't matter if you smoked or not; when you went in there, you smoked. And drank coffee. I had never had a cup of coffee in my life until I went to an AA meeting. Now I drink coffee all the time. But I'm okay with putting caffeine in my system. It's a lot better than some other things.

A little lady in our church named Cola Baker, an elder's wife, was instrumental in helping us start that group. Her brother was an alcoholic and she had always wanted a twelve-step group at a church. She was a tough old gal, almost like a Marine herself. She loved us old boys.

Cola taught us some eternal principles with daily living, just basic living stuff. But she was cool. She ended up helping a lot of people through her actions.

When she passed away, her family in Texas asked if I could preach at her funeral. There was a time in my life I couldn't imagine being asked to preach anywhere for anything. But God loves the ironies of life.

Another of the many ironies I would come to see was attending the same seminary that had brought my family to West Monroe in the first place, so my dad could study there.

In 1990 Mary and I decided we needed leadership training, so we committed ourselves to White's Ferry Road School of Biblical Studies for two years. It was an accredited biblical school where you studied Scripture and wrote papers. Since I had applied myself so well in high school and those brief few moments in college, seminary was more difficult for me than Mary. But I wanted to use my newfound passion for the Lord and was willing to do anything to grow in my walk with Him. So even though it was hard work, I ended up excelling in it (another wonderful God-inspired irony).

Overcomers Outreach and White's Ferry Road School of Biblical Studies taught me that God had room for anybody, and I mean anybody, in His ministry.

37

ALL THIS TIME

GATLINBURG is a small city in eastern Tennessee, high in the Smoky Mountains. It's a beautiful place to go on vacation and a tranquil setting to visit in the middle of summer. It's the perfect place to enjoy nature and learn that you have a brother your parents never told you about.

In the summer of 1991, we decided that it was time to tell the girls about Heath. Since Cherry was eleven, we had become concerned that she might meet her brother at a youth rally or even later in college. Having this blood connection, the two of them might have been drawn to each other and not even know why. We'd already seen strange things happen...like our sister-in-law staying *in Heath's house, in his bed!* We didn't want another call in the middle of the night.

"Mom, I just met the most amazing guy."

"What's his name, Cherry?"

"His name is Heath, and it seems like I've known him my entire life."

We already had a dramatic enough story.

It was time to do away with another secret.

It was a joy just walking downtown in this quaint little town and driving around the mountains looking at God's beautiful creation. The girls loved going to Ripley's Believe It Or Not! museum.

Then suddenly we found ourselves on the day. D-day.

Mac started the conversation, since I knew I couldn't do it. I would have started crying before I could get anything out.

"Before we leave for the day and have fun," Mac told Cherry and Callie, "let's sit down on the beds, 'cause we've got some things to tell you girls."

Cherry sat right down, already curious and so cute with her blonde curls and her hazel eyes. A matching pair of eyes had a hard time paying attention, as brown-haired Callie, seven and as rambunctious as ever, was eager to get going.

It was a moment I had feared and dreaded.

I'm going to see shock and disappointment on their faces, on the faces of the two brightest stars in our lives.

It was one thing to see my father's disappointment, or that of my family and friends, but our girls…

I don't want to tell them they don't need to know they can wait it can wait.

Mac's steady tone was reassuring.

"You know we've been trying to be open with you girls about things we've done. You know we've made a lot of mistakes in our lives. One of the things we have to tell you about is that you have a brother that we gave up for adoption."

Cherry and Callie were both listening attentively. I held my breath and tried to control my emotions as he spoke.

"We weren't married at the time, and it was wrong for us to have a baby together," Mac said. "We knew it would be better for the family, especially for Mamaw, if we didn't tell people about it. We wanted to find a better family for the baby to live in, a family that would love and provide for him the same way we do for you guys. So there was another couple who wanted a little baby, and they adopted your brother. We never had a chance to meet them, but we do know they're a loving Christian family."

"His name is Heath," I managed to say.

Cherry just stared at us for a moment, trying to take it in.

"We have a brother?" she said. "Well, when do we get to meet him?"

"That's great," Callie said. "Can we go swimming now?"

"Do you have any questions for us?"

They both shook their heads and said no, though Cherry looked as though she'd have to think about this information.

Both girls always had little wisps of curly hair around their sweet faces. I could never get it all contained in a ponytail. Their cousin Ryan said they looked like they had a lion's mane. I told him it was angel halos surrounding them.

All this time I had dreaded telling them. I had dreaded this moment. And now there they were—these two little angels on the beds, looking up at us with innocence and hope and love.

Later on, I told Mac that they were going to have to process this information. I was sure the questions would start later.

For the rest of the trip, every once in a while, one of them would ask a question about Heath...wondering what he looked like or how he acted or what it would be like to meet him. We didn't want to get their hopes up, yet we didn't want to squelch them either.

I couldn't tell them that just like the love I had for both of them was another love I'd kept hidden and imprisoned in a deep well inside of me. A love I'd held for the son we let go. I was afraid of letting it out because it had nowhere to go. I still didn't know if we'd ever meet Heath.

I still was unsure whether that love inside could grow.

God had already done so many amazing things in our lives. I couldn't demand or expect more, could I?

Yet I could ask and pray. That's all I could do. And I'd keep doing that for the son we'd never met and the brother Cherry and Callie now knew they had.

38

HOLD ON MY HEART

IN May of 1992, a gift came in the mail: a letter from the Arthurs, including another wallet-size picture of Heath. This time it was his high school graduation picture.

To say we were thrilled was an understatement. That worn-out photo of Heath from grade school was finally replaced. Yet it wasn't just seeing this picture. It was the fact that it came in the first place. It was a sign that maybe, just maybe, more would come.

It was still something Mary and I prayed for all the time, but I didn't really want to think about it or even talk about it much. It sounded too good to be true.

Barbara, our counselor friend who had talked to the Arthurs about us (sharing with them the details of my addiction in order to help Heath in the future), told us it would be appropriate to let the girls send Heath graduation gifts. They still often brought him up and asked about him. Mary had a great idea about filming the girls, letting him see them in person but from a safe distance. We didn't want to scare him off.

So we made a video, keeping it short and sweet, hoping it would intrigue Heath and make him want to meet his sisters. The girls were playing basketball, flying kites, and introducing themselves.

"Hi, my name is Cherry, and I'm twelve years old…"

"Hi, I'm Callie, and I'm almost nine…"

Cherry talked about her painting and the different things she was doing in school, while Callie talked about her toys and animals. It was fun, upbeat, and lighthearted. Mary wanted to put us at the end but didn't want to freak out Heath by saying a bunch of gushy stuff that might make him feel uncomfortable.

So instead we got Cherry to hold the video recorder and film us. We were sitting on the four-wheeler. We simply waved and drove off.

Mary hoped it would just whet his appetite and leave him wanting to know more about the four of us.

Turns out, Mary was right (she often tends to be). It also turns out I was wrong in doubting that we'd ever meet the son we gave up.

Some things are indeed too good to be true. But God is both. And He loves reminding us of this.

39

BABY, BABY

MOST people probably don't remember the first words they spoke to their newborn baby. But the first words I spoke to Heath are etched in my mind forever. Just like the moment I saw him. Just like the time I finally was able to hold him in my arms.

It had only taken nineteen years.

"Heath wants to meet us."

I almost dropped the phone. I couldn't believe what Mac was telling me.

"What? When?"

"The Arthurs just called and said Heath wants to meet us on his nineteenth birthday."

I was with my parents on a summer tradition we called the Grandkids Vacation. This year we were on a dude ranch in Bandera, Texas. We hadn't heard from the Arthurs since getting Heath's graduation picture two years before.

Now, as I held the pay phone receiver in my hands, I stood in disbelief.

"We're going to meet our son in two weeks," Mac said.

Two weeks…

It couldn't arrive soon enough. I'd waited so long, and yet now suddenly I wanted these next two weeks to be gone.

Another thought suddenly popped into my head.

We have to tell Mom.

We waited until we got home from the vacation, then Mac and I sat down at the kitchen table with my mother and father. We were all so nervous about it, wondering what she would say or do.

"Jean, we have something to tell you," Dad said.

My mom looked at us with excited eyes. "Are Mary and Mac going to have a baby?"

We all laughed.

"Well, it's kinda like that," Dad said with a grin. "Mary and Mac do have another baby."

Mom looked confused.

"Nineteen years ago, before they were married, Mary and Mac had a baby boy. They gave him up for adoption to a Christian couple who couldn't have children. And now we all are going to meet him next week! His name is Heath Arthur."

My mom laughed and said, "Oh, honey!" in her sweet southern drawl. "I'm so excited…but how did I not know about Mary having a baby back then?"

"That was before you were on this new medicine, and you weren't aware of things as you are now," Dad explained to her.

She just shook her head in amazement and kept laughing and smiling, so excited to hear about Heath. Mom was ready to meet him with the rest of us.

Mac and I left my parents' house in shock and thanksgiving at how good God is.

It was August 17, 1994.

That young couple riding around on a motorcycle seemed like a faint memory. The scared girl lying alone in the hospital bed seemed like a foggy dream. That drive home from Robeline to West Monroe seemed like a story from another life.

Yet those were memories and dreams and stories I'd still never fully dealt with. I'd never forgotten them. I'd never fully been able to tell my son farewell.

It turns out, I didn't have to.

I stayed busy and tried controlling my emotions, praying constantly. The smell of baking lasagna filled the house. A birthday cake decorated with baseball figures waited for Heath on the dining room table. Mac and I kept looking out the window at the driveway, waiting to see a vehicle, waiting to see the Arthurs driving up. Callie was outside jumping on the trampoline on the other side of the carport, bouncing higher than the hill that covered the road toward our house. She kept saying, "Not yet, not yet, not yet."

Suddenly an old blue Cadillac was rumbling down our driveway. Mom and Dad were soon at the window with us, watching as if Santa Claus was bringing us a midyear Christmas present he'd forgotten to hand off nineteen years earlier.

My heart could have propelled a jet airliner.

I looked at Mac for a moment, a smile of pure joy and astonishment on my face. "We're fixing to meet our son."

We were still those wide-eyed kids in love and disbelief at the gift God was giving us. After so long. After so many years. After so much had happened.

Lord, please don't let me faint or cry. Lord, help me stay strong.

I wanted Heath to enjoy meeting us. Since he was an only child, I didn't want all these people freaking him out. Especially a mother who looked half-deranged in her exuberance.

When the Arthurs got out of the car, his mother came first to me. She was a tall, older lady with tears covering her cheeks. She wrapped her arms around me and started talking and didn't stop. She made me feel very comfortable when she said in her charming Cajun accent, "Ah, it's so good to meet you."

Mr. Arthur was a tall, thin man with a real deep voice. He was very nice and polite as he greeted us.

Then there was Heath standing behind them.

It was one of the most surreal things I'd ever seen. There was this good-looking teenager who looked just like us. I immediately saw Mac's hands, his feet, and his hair. But Heath's mouth and his eyes were just like mine.

"Hi, Heath. I'm Mary."

He smiled and said, "Hi, Mary."

The Holy Spirit was keeping my emotions together. I smiled back, and then we hugged. I knew he could feel my shaking body as I held him and then as I looked into his eyes. Mac and the girls gave him hugs as well, and we talked with all of them in the driveway.

For what seemed like the longest time, I just stared at him. Eventually I apologized. "I'm sorry I keep staring, but I can't help it," I said.

This is so weird. And so wonderful.

Soon the girls were messing with Heath like typical teenagers might when meeting someone new. Mac had worried about entertaining Mr. Arthur and making him feel comfortable. Soon they were out on the front porch talking about all the different construction jobs they had been on while the girls and I oogled over Heath like he was a rock star who had suddenly come to the house.

The time evaporated that day. I loved watching Cherry and Callie interact with Heath, shooting hoops and bouncing on the trampoline.

Oh, I wish time would stand still.

It would have been easy to get melancholy, to imagine all the moments I missed.

Look what we gave up.

Look how far they have to go to get to know each other.

It would have been natural to go there.

But I didn't think those thoughts. Instead, I was grateful to God for allowing this miraculous moment to happen. I wanted to be truly thankful for where we were *on this day.* I wanted to be thankful for the *now.*

This was a great day. It felt natural and normal. Nothing felt strained or difficult. Heath was a delight to be around, and so were the Arthurs. There was never a moment where later I'd think, *Oh, boy, I stuck my foot in my mouth that time.*

God had answered our big prayer, and He also answered many small prayers, making sure all the little details were okay.

Isn't it great to have a God who cares about the big and the small? Who loves us enough to be concerned about every minute thing?

The love I felt for our newfound son was the same as I felt for Cherry and Callie. And it's only a drop in the ocean compared to the love God has for us.

As the day came to an end, we all agreed that we wanted to do this again.

How about tomorrow? was all I could think.

The Arthurs said we needed to come down and visit them. Soon enough we had made plans to see them again on Labor Day weekend. It wasn't just Mac and I who wanted to spend time with Heath. Now the girls loved him and wanted to be with him as well.

"I'll see you soon."

That was what I told Heath before the Arthurs left us after that first meeting on his birthday. I remember thinking of that young girl, so alone and so hopeless nineteen years before.

Nineteen long years. Gone. In a blink.

God knew. God had it all figured out. God had a plan.

That girl wasn't so young anymore, but neither was she alone, and she definitely wasn't hopeless. God had seen every one of her tears—for Mac, for her mother, for her regrets, for her girls, for Heath.

Today He was getting rid of that tear-filled bottle.

As I watched the Arthurs leave, I imagined that bottle drifting away in a vast, endless ocean.

No more tears. No more waiting. No more wondering.

"You've done more than I ever could imagine, God. I can't ask for more."

I didn't have to. God wasn't finished. God had a lot more plans for all of us.

PART THREE

THE SAME COMFORT

HE GIVES US

40

OUT IN THE WOODS

AFTER enough time spent in recovery, I started to be known as the guy you called when there were problems. One night, Phil Robertson and I got a call from a worried mother.

"My son Jimmy is out in the woods. He's hooked on gasoline. He's huffing the stuff and I don't know what to do. Do you think you guys could come and talk to him?"

Phil and I were happy to find someone else to share Jesus with, even if he was breathing in gas fumes.

We arrived at a nice house with a good-looking family; they seemed like any typical American family. The mother met us in the carport. She was friendly but clearly distressed.

"He's out there," she told us, gesturing toward the thick, menacing woods that surrounded their house.

"Can you give us an idea where?" I asked.

"Somewhere within a mile to a mile and a half just behind here," the mother said. "There's a pond out there somewhere."

Phil and I stared into the black forest. It was deathly silent. Then we looked back at each other and said, "All right then."

As we started to walk toward the woods, picking a random entry point, the mother called us back for a moment.

"One thing you have to know," she told us. "Jimmy's got a gun, but I don't think he'll shoot you."

I couldn't help laughing. At first I thought she was joking, then I realized she was serious.

"Is it a handgun?" I asked.

"No, it's a high-powered rifle, but I don't think he'd shoot y'all."

That's comforting...to know you don't think your gas-huffing son with the high-powered rifle somewhere in the big black woods will shoot us! Real comforting.

Phil and I kept walking toward the woods.

"Well, if we go in, we'll go out together," I said. "I don't know who he's going to take first."

We were walking in the dark forest for almost ten minutes when we started smelling gas. Maybe that was a clue. Then we noticed a pair of jeans in a tree. A shoe. A sock. Soon we reached a pond where we found the kid sitting in his underwear over a can of gas breathing in lungfuls.

We shouted out at him. "Jimmy, Jimmy!"

He looked up and for a moment acted like he was hearing things. "What are y'all doing here?"

Well, we're sure not duck hunting, Jimmy.

His rifle was leaning against a tree, so Phil and I stood casually between him and death.

"Why don't you come on back home with us?" Phil asked.

"Man, I got things to do," Jimmy's unsteady voice said.

Here was a kid, eighteen or nineteen years old, who'd taken his rifle and a can of gasoline out on a date. For some reason he'd decided to ditch all his clothes except for his tighty-whities, which weren't very tight anymore. It looked like Jimmy had been wearing them for several days. Actually he had a makeshift camp and didn't look like he was planning on going home anytime soon.

"Come on, Jimmy, come on back with us, man," I told him.

Phil and I joked with him and tried to reason and told him things could be okay.

Poor Jimmy was a pitiful sight, but I could've been Jimmy. I *was* once Jimmy.

We kept talking to him, but he never did come back out of the woods with us.

Jimmy was one of those who never did make it out of the darkness.

Unfortunately, there've been too many Jimmys. Way too many Jimmys.

It was just another reminder that I needed to stay strong, to never give up, to never stop giving everything over to God. And to definitely not get too sure in my recovery.

I could be back in the woods in a heartbeat. With one bad decision. With one stupid, selfish step.

The most dangerous moments in my recovery journey haven't been when I've been approaching a gasoline-huffing, rifle-toting kid in the woods. They've been when I've thought I'm different from him, that I'm better, that I'm beyond heading back into those woods myself.

41

ONE OF US

I enjoyed every moment I could getting to know Heath. Months after first meeting him, he started coming to our house quite often. We would stay up until two or three in the morning talking, me telling him about our life and Heath talking about his. It was impossible to fill in the gaps left by nineteen years, but we were certainly trying our best.

So one spring evening in 1995 while sitting on the steps outside our house, watching the sun slowly start to dip, Heath shared something that he'd been thinking about for some time.

"I'm tired of being a part-time brother. I want to be a full-time brother."

I was stunned, to say the least. "So what does that mean? What are you wanting to do?"

"I want to move up here," Heath said.

"You know we'd love that. But…you've got to really pray about it and think about how you're going to talk to your parents about this decision. Even though you're nineteen, you have to be careful. You don't want to hurt them."

Mac and I were always careful to refer to the Arthurs as Heath's parents. That's what they were and always would be. We never told him, "We're your mom and dad." And even though he understood this, he was still young and still figuring out thoughts and feelings he couldn't even begin to truly understand.

At this time he was attending the University of Southwestern Louisiana and, like so many other college students, had gotten into the party crowd and was starting to drink. He wasn't very serious about schoolwork or anything.

Whenever he came up to be around us, he would go to church and see how God had impacted our lives. This made a big difference to Heath. He felt like his life at USL was full of darkness, while anytime he came to West Monroe, he said he felt like there was light.

The more he came around, the more he realized this was where he needed to be.

Soon after that, he talked to his parents about moving up here before the next semester of school started. He wanted to stay in college as well as live with us.

It wasn't an easy decision for Heath or his parents. And it turned out it wasn't going to be easy on our family, either. We had gotten used to being a team of four. Suddenly we had an extra player in the mix. Regardless of how much we loved this new addition to our family, it was going to take a little while for us to get used to one another.

When you live in a big family, you all have to work together as a team. It's not about just any one person. We had chores and responsibilities, and suddenly there came Heath with no routine or responsibilities.

The reality was that Heath had grown up an only child and had been able to get away with a lot. So while we welcomed him to our home with open arms, it wasn't long until tensions started to surface, especially between him and Mac.

But another reality was this: Heath and Mac shared this unique link—the same DNA—so in a strange way both of them were thinking the same thing. Mac was dealing with this new son in his house, while Heath was dealing with this new father. Each of them had an idea of what that looked like, but those ideas didn't always match up.

The truth was this: I'm glad the Arthurs gave him so much love and attention. I'm glad Heath made the decision to move into our home and live for a while with us. I never thought I'd be given the gift of knowing him, but this was more than that. He was with us. And just as there is in any parent-child relationship, there were some tough times. We didn't have nineteen years to work on it. Everything was accelerated, and with Mac and Heath, things sometimes got heated. Both of them made mistakes.

But the devil wasn't going to have his way, not with this. Like everything in our lives, we decided to put it out there and talk about it. "There's some problems and we need to talk about them," Mac told him. "We don't just sweep things under the carpet."

I was nervous, because I didn't want this dream of ours that God had made come true to suddenly explode in anger and resentment. I tried to reason with Mac regarding Heath.

"Mac, we finally got him in our life. You've got to go easy. Be calm with him."

But Mac doesn't do anything halfway—partying or recovery or totem poles. So one day Mac came in and made an announcement. "I need counseling. And if I need counseling, we all need counseling."

So we went through counseling to talk about the issues we were all going through. It was good because I didn't want to burn any bridges with Heath. After living with us for a while, he came to see that we lived out the rest of the week what we heard preached on Sundays. He saw the gospel studies going on in our house and witnessed how people could come to know Jesus. Heath saw directly how lives were being changed, and we were fortunate to witness his spiritual birth in baptism.

God blessed our efforts, but it wasn't easy. Just like recovery, or just like dealing with life. Sometimes it's easy to look at the picture an artist unveils and marvel at how beautiful it looks. But what you don't see is the hard work and the endless amount of time that goes into creating that painting. It's easy to take that for granted unless you know how tough it was to finish.

I see our family like that. A colorful painting that is beautiful and flawed and never quite finished.

There's always something we're working on. Always.

42

BRAND NEW DAY

I love addicts. They can be the biggest-hearted people ever. They will give you the shirt off their back. But the problem with addicts is that when God was handing out emotions, we circled back around and got a double dose. That means we end up self-medicating to handle the extra emotions.

But addicts say the coolest things. One day I was sitting in a group with other men, and one of them said this: "I've been near the cross a lot of times in my recovery, but so were the guys who gambled for Jesus's clothes. I need to get near the Savior."

I was like *What? Wow.*

I met another guy through recovery who was down on his life. Things weren't going well for him. He came to our group and saw there could be hope. I asked him if he would like to know why my life had undergone such a dramatic change. He said yes, so I told him to come out to our house and I'd share it with him. When he came, I laid out the whole plan of God's salvation for him. He said he wanted Jesus to become Lord of his life. I explained to him how in the New Testament this was always followed by baptism. So I asked if he would like to be baptized.

In his excitement he shouted, "Hell yeah, I'm ready!"

I told him, "Really, we're trying to keep you out of hell."

You hear some of the coolest things in recovery because, man, these people are broken. They have nowhere else to go and they aren't trying to impress anybody.

There was a rough, hardworking ironworker in his early thirties that I led to Jesus. Since he didn't have any biblical knowledge, he asked me if I would meet with him to study the Bible. But this was the test to see if he really wanted it—I told him I would meet with him at six o'clock every Tuesday morning. When he showed up, I knew he was serious.

Around that same time, I led a doctor of marriage and family therapy to the Lord as well. He too wanted to learn more about the Bible, so I told him I would meet him on Thursday mornings at six. It wasn't long before the Tuesday guy heard about the Thursday guy and asked if he could come on that day as well.

That's how our Tuesday/Thursday Bible studies were born.

For the next ten years, the doctor was bringing therapists and the ironworker was bringing addicts. Eventually the head of the marriage and family program at the local college began coming to our morning studies.

One morning we were studying 2 Thessalonians 1:8, where it says that Jesus will punish those that don't know God. This man, who has more degrees than he can even remember, said, "Stop!" in the middle of our discussion. I was a little taken aback.

The doctor's eyes were wide and curious. "Who's going to punish those that don't know God? I thought it was Satan."

"No, it says here that the one who punishes those that don't know God will be Jesus," I told him.

"This is pressing business," he said in a very strong voice. "Carry on!"

He stayed late that morning because he wanted to hear the rest of the story, and became convinced that Jesus had to be a part of his life. He came to many more Bible studies and meals at our home because he was hungry to know more.

So the dynamics were very interesting in our early morning groups, with addicts, who are very manipulative, trying to manipulate the doctors, and the doctors, who want to fix everybody, trying to fix the addicts. On many occasions I had to remind them both that this was about their own spiritual growth. Over the next ten years many men in that group came to faith in Christ.

Mary used to say that Tuesdays and Thursdays were her favorite mornings. "When I look out in the morning and see our yard covered in trucks and cars," she said, "I know these are men who are wanting to be more godly and lead their families in a better way."

They were learning "GOD"...an acrostic for Good Orderly Direction.

The Bible studies got so big they had to move out of the office into the cabinet shop. Thirty to forty men were driving all the way out to our house before the sun rose. Sometimes we would still be in bed and we'd see headlights in our driveway. (But there was quite a difference between seeing those headlights and seeing the ones belonging to cops investigating a report of a naked guy roaming around a trailer park!)

I used to be the first one there, around 5:30, to make the coffee and get everything ready. But then some guys started getting there at 5:25 so they could beat me. So the next time I'd show up at 5:15, then they would show up the next morning at 5:10. When they started showing up at 5:00, I declared them the winner. I wasn't getting up any earlier than that.

But remember—I only had to walk down to the shop from the house. Some of these guys were getting up at 4:00 a.m. just to get there that early.

As the Bible studies grew, there were many days when someone would say, "I really want to be baptized right now." So we would all go down to the lake, check for water moccasins and alligators, clear the moss, walk out into the water, and bury them in baptism out in the swamp. Mary would bring towels from the house to dry them off. I kept a supply of old shorts and T-shirts at the shop ready to go.

A simple connection and desire to grow in the Word resulted in a movement where God was working mightily. I never imagined those Tuesday and Thursday mornings could grow into something so large and joyous. But the Spirit was at work. In all areas of our lives.

In 1995, when I was thirty-seven years old, I had the great privilege of being ordained as an elder at White's Ferry Road, along with Phil Robertson. All the elders stood around us, laying their hands on us and praying. I could never have imagined this moment in my younger years. I could see the tears on Mary's face. I was proud too. I happened to be the youngest elder in our church's fifty-year history. And, I would remind myself, lest I get too full of myself, the only one who was a former meth addict.

On Sunday nights we had house church—smaller, more intimate groups that met in different members' homes rather than gathering as one congregation back at the church building. Our friendship with the Robertsons continued to grow, just like our ministry, and we eventually started a house church with Phil and Kay. I was asked to be the worship leader—talk about getting somebody that makes a joyful noise! Within a couple of years, we had to birth another house church because it had gotten so big. Mary and I were the logical choice to take the new group, even though we didn't want to. We enjoyed being at the Robertsons'. But we took this new group of about twenty and moved to our house. Within a couple of years, we were up to over eighty people every Sunday night. We knew we were getting too big when there were separate conversations going on in the back of our living room while I was teaching a lesson. Over the years three different house churches were birthed out of our home church.

One of the highlights of every Sunday evening came when house church was over. Along with all the other fathers, I would take the kids fishing in the lake behind our house. We would run what are called yo-yos. These are probably only legal in Louisiana, where pretty much any method to catch wild game is legit.

A yo-yo is a round device about the size of a kid's yo-yo. The difference is it has a spring in the middle. You pull the string out, set a little catch in a notch in the side of the yo-yo, and have a hook and bait on the other end of the string. When a fish bites the bait, it releases the catch and reels the fish to the top of the water. So on Sunday afternoons before house church, I would go out and bait all the yo-yos. And after house church we would get into boats with all the kids and take spotlights to see what the yo-yos had caught.

The kids had a blast taking the fish off the yo-yos and throwing them in the bottom of the boat. The only thing that would stop them was seeing the bright-red eyes of an alligator gar glowing in their spotlight. All the kids would get to the back of the boat in a hurry after seeing those rows and rows of sharp teeth...they were afraid the gar would get them just like the fish got their bait.

Those couple of hours of good, clean fun are more memorable to me now than any of the drug-fueled parties I used to have. The connections and relationships mattered. And we were all together for one purpose: to worship God.

Nobody says you can't have laughter and joy and hunting all while gathering together to worship our Lord.

43

ONLY TIME

SOME days seem dark and endless and depleting. Then others are bright and brilliant and gone before you realize they even began. But those are the days you find yourself thinking back on with a smile on your lips and thanks-giving in your heart.

I blinked, and before I knew it, my babies were all grown up and gone.

June 1, 1996. I walk down the aisle with Heath's mother on one side of him and me on the other. Mac and Heath's father await us at the end of the aisle.

All those prayers that Heath would meet the perfect girl, offered up before God from the moment he was born...God heard them and gave us Carmen. She is the right and perfect one for Heath. They look at one another with star-filled eyes of hope. Hope for the two of them. Hope for all of us.

And hope for three perfect gifts one day: three beautiful grandchildren named Caroline, Gannon, and Anna Kate.

All from the son we didn't know and didn't ever think we'd even meet.

All from a God who hadn't forgotten about those prayers and didn't let us spend the rest of our lives wondering and waiting.

November 18, 2000. The joy that came as a blessing and a gift and a miracle is finally all grown up. Daddy's first little girl is getting married. It seems like Cherry has been a part of our lives for as long as we could remember. Yet it also seems like she's leaving far too soon.

We've been through the diapers and heard her first word of "Dada." We saw her learn to walk with her hands held up high in the air and watched her leave us on the first day of kindergarten.

Those school projects (hello, totem pole!) and the sports and the best girlfriends and the boys suddenly entering the picture. Boys who didn't seem to stand out until Josh came and gently took her heart.

November 18 was also the first day of duck season. Mac and Josh couldn't believe we scheduled the wedding this day, while we couldn't believe they actually had to go hunting (well, maybe we could believe it). But they promised us they would be in early, and true to their word, the groom-to-be and his future father-in-law were there right on time.

A sea of pink bridesmaids gowns glide between the black tuxes of the groomsmen. Everything is planned down to the minutest details, including a totem-pole-esque archway Mac has built, covered in white tulle and twinkle lights.

Everything is planned, that is, except my heart stopping the moment I see Cherry walking under that archway with her father.

In her Cinderella bridal gown with a tiara on the top of her head, she truly looks like an angel floating down the aisle. Mac performs the ceremony, sharing special memories about Cherry as a child and Josh winning her heart.

God surely smiles, too, knowing that in five years, this exuberant couple will be blessed by handsome twin boys, Jett and Owen.

May 28, 2005. Another blink, and Callie is all grown up and starting a whole new chapter in her life.

I think back to our little baby, the one who talked us into getting so many pets throughout the years—rabbits, pygmy goats, a potbellied pig, a horse named Dixie, cats and hedgehogs and countless dogs. Her favorite was a blue heeler named Sassy who was part of our lives for fourteen years. Callie has always been a nurturer.

I think of the day Mac baptized her at a worship service. Seeing her born as a baby and then born again in Christ was something we cherished with each of the children.

We're all lined on a Destin beach with emerald-green waves crashing up behind Jacob, Mac, and the groomsmen. The groom's eyes are glued on Callie as she walks toward him. I'll never forget the look on Jacob's face as he watches Callie walk down a sandy aisle. She looks like a princess in her fairy-tale bridal gown, walking down a sand dune with her big brother, Heath, giving her away while Mac performs the ceremony.

I take a deep breath and enjoy the moment.

Callie and Jacob share hearts full of hope and longing for new adventures.

And again, nobody can know the hope and adventures that will arrive in Solomon, Silar, and Sayla-Jewell.

Nobody except God, of course.

Mac and I were so proud as we watched our three children pledging themselves to their spouses before God, our family, and friends. We love thinking about our legacy of faith in God being carried on from generation to generation until Jesus comes back.

In those dark moments of despair during Mac's addictions, I couldn't imagine days such as these. But God was merciful.

I blink and hold on to the joy of these days, and the promise from Isaiah 59:21: "'As for me, this is my covenant with them,' says the Lord. 'My Spirit, who is on you, will not depart from you, and my words that I have put in your mouth will always be on your lips, on the lips of your children and on the lips of their descendants—from this time on and forever,' says the Lord."

44

CHANGE THE WORLD

MARY'S brother, Johnny, was the first one to tell us about Celebrate Recovery. He had been out at Saddleback Church in California (Rick Warren's church) and came back with a gift for us.

"There's a really cool recovery ministry out there at the Saddleback. You should check it out," Johnny said. "I brought you one of their starter kits."

We're doing recovery already, and we're doing a pretty good job of it.

This was my thought. I thanked him and said I appreciated it, but my true thoughts were something more along the lines of *How dare you think we need help?*

But Johnny kept bugging us about going to California to check it out.

We had been working in Overcomers Outreach at White's Ferry for over fifteen years, a ministry that became our church's largest local outreach. Those years were really a great thing for Mary and me because they helped us get our feet on the ground. We got to meet and minister to hundreds of people who came seeking relief from their alcoholism and drug addictions. Many even became leaders in Overcomers and in the church.

Looking back now, the only problem I would say about Overcomers Outreach was the fact that it segregates. While it was a good and very easy group to lead, it was strictly for drug addicts and alcoholics and their family members. And any time we segregate sins within the church, we're in danger of excluding people who need help.

Those fifteen years were about helping others and at the same time building this tremendous base for what would become Celebrate Recovery. We already had a staff of leaders ready and able, people who could move in and start Step Studies and lead Open Share groups.

The timing was right. But standing in the way was Mac Owen. A totem pole of pride.

I learned early in my recovery from my sponsor in AA that this type of thinking is called "contempt prior to investigation." On page 568 of the Big Book of Alcoholics Anonymous, it says this is a principle that will keep a person in everlasting ignorance. In other words, if you think you know everything, you'll never learn anything.

So when I finally admitted that it was my pride getting in the way, I decided we would go to Southern California to check out this thing called Celebrate Recovery.

It's going to be cool 'cause they're paying our way and we can explore Southern California.

If I had to be truly honest, that's what was going through my mind. I still didn't really want to check it out in earnest. I just wanted to be able to say we had.

Well, remember when I did that for Overcomers Outreach? Thinking I should tell our church about it, but never really thinking that it would be anything more, and especially not thinking *I'd* be a part of it?

So Mary and I went to Saddleback Church in August of 2004 for their Celebrate Recovery Summit. The three-day conference is designed to help churches start a Celebrate Recovery program of their own or gather tips on improving existing programs. It didn't start until nine or nine thirty, but we got there at eight o'clock. I was thinking we could arrive early and leave early, maybe around eleven, and go to Laguna Beach.

We left at nine o'clock that night.

All throughout the day, one thing after another made us stop and think, *Wow, that's pretty cool.* Like the testimonies, for instance. There was this one guy who got up before everybody and shared that he struggled with sexual addiction. Mary and I had never even heard the word *sex* spoken in front of everybody in a church setting, but there was this man, sharing his story with peace and hope. We were amazed to hear someone like this sharing his struggles and also sharing his victory over them.

We wanted to hear more. Lots more.

By the end of the first day, I had to fess up to Mary.

"Shame on me," I said. "Really, this is some pretty good stuff. We can use some of this in conjunction with what we already do."

So even then, after a whole day of listening and learning, I was still saying, *Yeah, it's good but we still know some stuff.* Like I was actually hoping they'd call me up there to speak, just so I could tell them what we had going on down in West Monroe, Louisiana.

Well, God needed to work on me a little longer.

The next day we arrived at eight again because I was still deadset on leaving early and exploring Southern California.

This is good stuff and we'll use it and help people...but I want to see the ocean!

On our second day, we ended up leaving at ten. At night.

Those fourteen hours were awesome, including the concert in the evening. There were plenty of opportunities for Mary and me to leave, but by the end of the day I had other ideas.

God had finally gotten through.

We had met the founder of CR, John Baker, along with his wife, Cheryl. Before we left, I went up to Cheryl and said, "Well, we're stopping what we're doing, and we're doing this."

She said, "Okay" with a lot of uncertainty.

She wasn't used to my intensity. Or my big hair.

Mary and I decided to follow the book. There was no sense in trying to reinvent Celebrate Recovery, since it appeared it was working for so many other churches. They have a ninety-day kickoff plan, so we decided to do that. Only ours lasted a hundred and twenty days. I like to joke and say it's because we're a little bit slower than other folks, but in reality it's because we wanted to be thorough about it.

Also because I really wanted to start on New Year's Eve. And that was only a month away.

So we started our Celebrate Recovery in West Monroe with a party. And that became a tradition—having a CR party every New Year's Eve, even if it didn't fall on a meeting day. Because that's a safe place to go.

A few years later Mary had another idea: "Why don't we have the party at a skating rink?"

"A skating rink?" I asked, thinking, *That's probably one of the dumbest ideas I've heard.*

Contempt prior to investigation, Mac, contempt prior to investigation!

"If you can talk the rest into it, that's fine with me," I said.

So Mary, being sweet Mary, told everybody, "We're going to have a skating rink party on New Year's Eve."

It was one of the best decisions we ever made for New Year's Eve. Seeing a bunch of ex-addicts who still think they can skate get out there in a roller rink was priceless. It was hilarious and so much fun.

We started Celebrate Recovery on New Year's Eve, and we still meet fifty-two Friday nights a year. Once, when

CR fell on Christmas Day, some of the pastors and elders of the church asked if we were going to let people off for Christmas.

I said, "Man, no. Our addictions never took off during the holidays. They just got worse."

That's one of the many things I love about Celebrate Recovery. It's the intensity and the intentionality. It's saying, "We're going to be there. We made a commitment."

It's hard to think of any other ministry I've been a part of that is as intentional as that. When Christmas Day is on a Sunday or a Wednesday night, we'll cancel regular church services in a minute. But Celebrate Recovery will be there because there are always hurting people who need a place to be on those days.

I told myself I didn't need rehab, but Mary had already packed my suitcase in the trunk. I told myself the church didn't need Overcomers Outreach, but the elders asked how soon we would start. I told myself we didn't need Celebrate Recovery, but God showed me that, once again, Mac Owen was wrong.

Mary and I began our ministry with Celebrate Recovery on New Year's Eve, 2004. Nine years later, we can't imagine our lives without our Forever Family. But even then, we still only saw the small picture. God had larger plans for us. Much larger plans.

He always does if you let Him.

45

HAVE A CIGAR

IN August of 2005, Cherry and Josh were blessed to have twin sons. Mac and Josh were building their family a house next door to ours while they lived on our land in a trailer across the street. After a few months of my being over there all the time, we just had Cherry and Josh and the twins move in with us until their house was finished.

We don't remember much about the rest of that year!

46

HOW CAN I KEEP FROM SINGING?

MY father was about to die, and he knew it.

It was the last week of October 2006.

When my father was in his thirties, he often got walking pneumonia as well as dealing with allergies caused from secondhand smoke in the offices and boardrooms in which he spent all his time. I can remember these places well from the time I was small, because no matter what he was doing at the time, I was allowed to come in and see him. Those rooms were like AA meetings, thick with smoke. Since my father never slowed down or rested, nor went to the doctor, he didn't realize his lungs were getting scarred. Big pockets were forming in his lungs, and he ended up getting a fungus. His doctor told him he needed to move to Arizona, but my father wouldn't hear of it. Louisiana was where all his family lived and the home of the church he had helped start.

Over the years he tried many different breathing treatments, but eventually the doctor said, "Your lungs are in bad shape. You really need a lung transplant."

It was a dangerous proposition, since both of his lungs were so scarred.

"If you had one healthy lung, we could transplant the other, and you could still live if the new one didn't work," the doctor said. "But since both lungs are so bad, if one doesn't make it through the surgery you're doing to die."

So my father just got progressively worse, until at the end of his life his lungs filled up with fluid and basically drowned him. Hospice administered morphine to him daily. They said they could come in every day and do it, or a family member could act as his "nurse." So I told them I'd do it.

I moved in with my parents. The doctors said he might live two weeks or two months or six months—they weren't sure. Our goal was simply to make him as comfortable as possible.

My brother and sister asked if I could do this.

"Well, we'll take it one day at a time," I told them. "I know I can do it today, so let's go with it."

You were the first man to come into my life. I always felt safe with you. You held me in your strong and gentle hands when I was a baby—wrapped your arms around me and gave me big bear hugs when I was a little girl—held my hand as you walked me down the aisle in my wedding—and lifted me down into the water to be baptized and arise a new person. I have always had total trust in your arms.

Two days before Dad passed away, the hospice nurse came in the morning and gave him a sponge bath. After she was gone, I noticed how dry his feet looked. So I took some lotion and gently massaged his feet. As I did this, Isaiah 52:7 came to my mind. "How beautiful on the mountains are the feet of those who bring good news, who proclaim peace, who bring good tidings, who proclaim salvation, who say to Zion, 'Your God reigns!'"

The hymnals my father helped create and publish had sold more than three million copies worldwide. So many songs full of good news and peace and tidings, shared with so many people. So many hymns proclaiming the glory of God and how He reigned.

I looked at Dad's tired and weary body and knew God was calling him beautiful!

God was also saying in a calm whisper in my father's ear, "Not much longer, Alton Howard, my good and faithful servant. Not much longer."

At the end of your workday you would pull into the driveway and Janice and I would run to you, begging to ride on the hood of the car. We never worried if we could get hurt, because our daddy's hands were in control of the wheel. Once the car stopped, we would jump off the hood into your arms over and over again while squealing, "Happy days are here again. Yea!"

You always worked hard with your hands to take care of us. You took care of others by giving of your time, your energy, and your money. You used your hands to teach us how to catch fish—and how to clean them, cook them, and eat them—and to enjoy the crispy tails.

That day before I washed his feet, I got my father to sit up in his recliner and I trimmed his hair. He had started to look like a wild-haired Albert Einstein. He was still talking at this time, telling me he knew his time on this earth was getting close to the end. At one point, his eyes teared up as he was talking.

"I'm not done writing everything I want to write," he said. "There's a lot more I can say to encourage others of all God can do in their lives."

My father had just helped publish a book called *Witness* that I cowrote with Debbie Webb. We were able to show it to Dad before he passed. He was also still working on a book called *Morsels for the Road*, which he described as "tidbits of encouragement and hope for anyone with a hurt, hang-up, or habit." In other words, any member of the human race. Even though his body was failing him, his mind was strong to the end as he challenged and encouraged us through his faith and hope in Jesus.

I held my father's hands and looked in his eyes.

"Dad, you have taught us and countless other people how to live here for the next life to come. We have learned so many lessons through your teachings and your life. You have prepared us well to carry the baton forward."

Then I started singing "Victory in Jesus," one of his

favorite songs. He used to lead our church family in that hymn on Sunday mornings. I sang it with conviction while combing his hair. We used to sing together, harmonizing our voices while he played the piano, but this time he was too weak. So he sat there quietly with his eyes closed listening to me sing, and he was smiling so big. Then I kissed him gently, lingering with that kiss on his forehead, the man who had kissed my hurts my entire life.

I loved that moment with him. I could feel God's presence all around us giving us both comfort.

You used your hands in making up funny antics to make us giggle—remember the laughing game? Playing the piano and guitar, you were always creating new songs and funny words—remember the laughing song? Notice how your games and songs all have the word laughing in them. You delighted in making us laugh!

All the fun memories of hoedowns during the holidays and any other occasion you could talk us into playing musical instruments. Johnny playing the guitar, me playing the violin, along with Ryan, Cherry, Callie—we would make you beam with joy. We have all stood around the piano so many times while you played and we sang—church songs, Christmas songs, and just plain good ole country songs.

Once he knew he didn't have much longer to live, my father was determined that he and Mom would downsize before he went.

"We've got to get your mother out of this big house, because if I die here, you're going to have a hard time getting her out."

So two weeks before he died—while he was in the hospital—Dad told us, "Put the house up for sale. Get everything out as much as you can. Y'all divide it between you and put as much as you can in a double-wide for me and Mom."

So we got that done and got him moved home, and a week later he died.

Mac reflected on this recently. With an ironic chuckle he said, "Here's a man who literally made millions in his life, then downsized to a double-wide trailer and was perfectly content."

We watched you share the gospel with countless people out of your deep conviction and love for the Lord. We watched you lead the singing at church with your hands lifted high in the air—tapping your foot to the beat. You loved to change things up to keep the mood fresh and alive—pointing to different sections of the congregation for their next part to sing.

One day at noontime, Dad quit talking. It was almost as if he went unconscious. I called the hospice nurse and told her what had happened.

"I just want you to know this, that he can hear," the nurse told me. "We really believe people hear up until their last breath. So tell your family members when they come that he hears what they say."

We started telling all the family so they would come in and talk to him. It was so sweet, everybody coming in. I thought to myself, *Everybody needs to come see him because we don't know how long he's going to last.*

I asked Mac to come and stay with me because I knew I couldn't do this by myself. I needed my totem pole of strength at my side to see me through this time.

Mac came and made a big pot of gumbo that day. That trailer smelled so warm and inviting. I was worried that Dad was starving, but the nurse told me that once the body was preparing itself to die, it begins to shut down. So that included not wanting food anymore, even Mac's gumbo. The doctors said, "Don't force food on him. If he wants to eat, okay, but don't worry because he's preparing for the next step."

Dad's bed was in the den. Initially, when he came home from the hospital, we had his hospital bed set up in a bedroom. But he said, "No, no, no, I want to be in the den where everybody is. You put my bed right in the middle of the den."

So we said, "Okay, Dad," and installed him right in the middle of the den. Mac had been staying there the last few nights, so he would sleep on the couch and there was Dad right beside him. Since it was a mobile home, it was very tight inside.

At eleven o'clock that night, I gave Dad his morphine through his breathing treatment. The morphine came in little drops, and Dad would breathe it in his mouth. They were giving him that because they said since liquid was filling up his lungs, he could have a very violent death if he wasn't calm. It could be very scary.

That night, after the breathing treatment was over, I sat there knowing these might be the last words I ever spoke to my father. Here we were in this small trailer, just Dad and Mom along with Mac and me.

It still seemed like yesterday when I was a teenager and knelt by his side to tell him the news. All this time and all these years and all those answered prayers, yet life still stung. Life still hurt. Especially seeing him struggling to stay alive.

"Dad, I love you," I said in a calm voice. "You know it's okay for you to go on if you want to. You've done everything to prepare all of us for heaven, so it's okay if you go."

Dad hadn't said a word or even made a single expression or movement since noon. But as soon as I said those words and told him "I love you, Daddy," his eyebrows went up.

He heard me. He knew we loved him and that it was okay to go.

I kissed him and then stood up and went to the bedroom in the back. I knew I needed some rest because I wasn't sure how long this was going to take or how difficult things might get for Dad and for all of us.

Your love for beautiful flowers helped us grow up appreciating the beauty of the great outdoors. I remember all those times we went to Bellingrath Gardens in Mobile to bring home a whole carload of flowers to plant in our yard. And all the trips you drove for Grandkids Vacation: Silver Dollar City, Disney World, Grand Canyon, skiing in Colorado, the dude ranch in Bandera. We have so many happy memories of the great outdoors with you and Mamaw.

And most importantly, you set such an example in the way you have always loved our mother. The way you and Mom take care of each other is so sweet. The way you call her queenie and she calls you honey. Seeing the sparkle in your eyes as you enjoy your grandchildren and great-grandchildren—feeding the ducks with them—bird-watching—squirrel hunting—playing "Bear Fly" and "Are You a Monkey?" with them. We love you, Dad, and are so grateful for the legacy you have established. We are committed to carrying it forward.

At 3 a.m. I was awakened by what I believe was an angel. I felt a nudge, physical or spiritual or something, and I bolted up in my bed. I just knew.

He's gone. Daddy's gone.

So I stood up and ran into the den, and it was total peace and quiet in there. Mac was asleep and my father was just lying there with his hands folded and his mouth barely open in a relaxed way. I knelt down and rested my head against his chest. There was no heartbeat. But he was still warm.

I knew he had just left.

I woke up Mac and asked him if he had heard anything, but Mac said no.

Once again, God had answered a prayer. I had asked God that Dad would go in peace. A lot of people had warned us to be prepared since it could be very violent and scary in those last few moments. But for Dad, it was quiet and calm and peaceful. Just like he was.

He had simply stopped breathing and gone to be with the Lord.

I didn't want to wake my mother up since she was sleeping in the other room, so Mac and I went outside the trailer, and I just cried and cried. For a long time Mac held me in his arms while I wept.

We decided to wait to call my brother and sister so they could sleep a little while longer too. We called them at six that Sunday morning to tell them Dad was worshiping the Lord in heaven.

I wondered what it was like for my father, the musician and songwriter, to finally hear the hosts of angels singing in the heavens. Imagine the orchestras and symphonies and the glorious music they were all making.

I thought of something else. My father's last words to Mac and me. "I'll see you in the new heaven and the new earth."

He didn't worry about where he was going. He didn't wonder what was coming next. He held this beautiful, brilliant thing called hope in his hands and his heart. He not only took it home with him, but he reminded all of those around him about it. Just as he had done his entire life.

I'll see you soon, Dad.

47

TEN YEARS GONE

THANK *God it's Monday.*

This is what Sam used to think when waking up at the start of a workweek. This is what he said to himself as he took that first drink, the first of many. He would finish the day and eventually pass out blind drunk, trying to forget his troubles and trying to wash away his pain.

He drank to ease his contempt of his colleagues. He drank to try to steady his confusion and hatred at the hypocrisy he saw daily. The only grace he could find was in this weekly routine at the bottom of a vodka bottle.

Sam was like anybody else, just living life, dealing with the hurts and the habits and the hang-ups that come with it. The only difference was Sam had been a pastor for forty years.

The sad truth is that churches can be brutal on preachers. The churches Sam preached for were so pharisaical that he could never live up to their standards. The irony was they couldn't, either!

For a decade, his Monday appointment with drunken oblivion had been taking place, and nobody knew except his wife. He hated living a lie, and eventually he couldn't take it anymore. One day Sam took a handful of pills along with that bottle of vodka. Thankfully, God spared Pastor Sam's life.

I was fortunate to get the call to go visit him.

As I sat in the intensive care unit at the hospital, I prayed over Sam. Here was a man Mary and I didn't know personally, a man in his seventies who had decided to throw away the most precious gift God had given him: his life.

"Don't give up, Sam," I told him. "God still has a plan for you."

Sam made it through ICU and eventually got out of the hospital. No longer a pastor, he was suddenly one of "those people." He started to go to Overcomers with me at a rehab facility called Rays of Sonshine. He also came to the Bible studies on Tuesday and Thursday mornings. Sam never missed Celebrate Recovery meetings. After being in ministry so many years, he was now in recovery, leaning on God's strength and looking to me to show him the way.

We were known for being the recovery church in our community—a church full of "those people." If church leaders had problems with their members and sent them to us, we welcomed them with open arms. We were there and we just wanted to love them. Sam and his wife became members of our church family.

So that's the end of the story about Pastor Sam, right? Another amazing story of how someone in the ministry, someone doing the same thing for so many years, could still have his heart broken and then put back together with God's help.

Yes, it's an amazing story. But there's one more interesting little tidbit.

One night at a small group, Sam shared with me that he had just met Heath's parents at church the past Sunday.

I nodded and laughed. "Sam, everybody has," I told him. "The Arthurs go to church here now!"

Along with Heath, the Arthurs had decided to move up to West Monroe and were now attending church with us. Everybody knew our story. But it turns out Pastor Sam knew another part of it.

"No, no, you don't understand," Sam said. "Forty years ago, when I first became a pastor, I performed the Arthurs' marriage ceremony."

For a moment I just stared at him.

Even before Mary and I got together and before Heath was born, God had a plan. God used Sam to marry the couple who in years to come would adopt our son. And then, in a amazing twist, God allowed me to be instrumental in giving Sam the hope that his relationship with God could not only be restored, but God would continue to use him.

Whether you're a young Mac Owen or an old Pastor Sam or somewhere in the middle, let me encourage you to hang on. God always sees the big picture, and He's always right on time.

48

CLIMB EV'RY MOUNTAIN

IMAGINE telling all your secrets and sorrows in front of a sanctuary of several thousand people.

Imagine if you weren't used to speaking in front of a lot of people, and if telling your story still brought tears to your eyes and weight to your soul.

Imagine sharing all the hurts you'd gone through and the healing God had given.

Imagine doing this with your best friend who had gone through the same hurts and had been the cause of many of them.

I didn't have to imagine, because soon Mac and I were standing in front of a bunch of smiling strangers and telling our story.

It was a simple story really. Just a story about a girl who fell for a boy. About mistakes made and about a life we tried to build on our own. About how Satan tried his best to tear every good thing apart, but how God won. How things weren't perfect and never would be, but how through the darkness came light and hope.

A simple story, just like every simple story of God saving lives.

Simple, that is, unless you're the star of that story. Simple unless you're the one God saves.

It's amazing to think about that trip Mac and I took to California to check out Celebrate Recovery. At that time, neither of us expected to suddenly change what we were doing and dive into this ministry. Yet only a few years later, we could hardly remember what life was like without CR and our Forever Family. The more we became involved, the more opportunities opened up for us...

As time went by, it became obvious that Mac and I should share our testimony publicly. This was easy for Mac—from his very first days in rehab, he was used to sharing about himself and his addictions. But I grew up in a church where women never spoke in public, so the thought of getting up before a CR group was the furthest thing from my mind.

We finally began working on our joint testimony for Celebrate Recovery and because we were CR State Reps we were asked to send it in to CR Founder John Baker.

We were surprised when he sent it back to us and asked us to cut its length. So we did, and then he asked us to cut it again. And again. He made us edit down our story four times!

For time's sake, out went some of the important details. The African-American nurse at Heath's delivery. My miscarriage. Other details that we couldn't fully get into because they simply took too much time.

In the summer of 2007, we gave our testimony twice during a Free Indeed tour to South Africa. Free Indeed is an a capella contemporary Christian music ministry. They asked Mac and me to help with the spiritual aspect of the trip, leading daily devotionals and sharing about Celebrate Recovery. We eventually gave our testimony a few more times at CR meetings and even at two of CR's One Day leadership training seminars, the first in New Orleans and the second time in Oklahoma City.

After the second time, John Baker came up to us with this grin on his face—the little grin that lets you know something is up.

"Cheryl has something to tell you," John said, clearly about to burst with his news.

Eventually Cheryl told us what they were thinking. "We'd like you to share your testimony at the Summit."

The same Summit Mac and I had attended in 2004. The one at Saddleback Church that leaders from all over the country attend. The thought of speaking in front of three or four thousand people gave me a near heart attack. Could she be serious?

"There's a catch," Cheryl said.

Uh-oh.

"I want your whole family to come," Cheryl said. "What I see is you guys introducing your family members, since they are also involved in Celebrate Recovery. And then introducing your son."

I took a deep breath and held it in. For a long time.

By this time, Mac and I were secure in our relationship with Heath. We knew he would be willing to do it.

So we agreed to ask the children what they thought. Soon everybody was on board and eagerly awaiting the Summit that summer.

The main worship hall of Saddleback Church looked a lot larger from the platform we stood on. Much like the day when we first met Heath, I was praying fervently for God to hold back my emotions and tears.

Yet as Mac started to talk, I could feel the tears coming on.

"Hi, I'm a believer in Jesus Christ who has struggled with drugs and alcohol for much of my life. My name is Mac. I am able to say *much* of my life instead of *most* of my life because of Jesus. I lived to see a milestone in my recovery. After over twenty years in recovery, I have been sober longer than I was using."

The smiles and the applause soothed my soul. After a few moments of standing there listening to Mac talk and make the crowd laugh, I was reminded that we had found a family in Celebrate Recovery. We had found a home. A safe place.

I had my words memorized, and all I tried to do was articulate them without fumbling up with sadness or emotion.

"As they rushed me into the delivery room, a nurse

shoved a gas mask over my face. I thought they were suffocating me to punish me for what I had done."

Every time I thought it would be too much to keep going, the laughter, the tears, and the applause would urge me on. After sharing about giving up our baby and then being sent to a Christian college out of state where "my dad was hoping to get me away from Mac," there was laughter, and then Mac paused for effect.

"But I followed..."

More laughter and louder applause.

It felt so good to be able to share with all these people the hope Mac and I had in our hearts. I could see their faces and could see the hands wiping the tears out of their eyes. It felt good to share the verses that had carried me like a life raft of hope in a dark ocean of doubt.

"My feeble prayer at the time was that Mac would just stay awake in church and hear the message. Never in my wildest dreams was I thinking of bigger things—like Mac becoming an elder in our church or starting a CR ministry there or becoming the CR Louisiana State Rep."

The applause stopped me from continuing on for a few moments.

"The only reason I share these things with you is to confirm that God takes broken lives and does exceedingly more than we can ask or imagine!"

We didn't want to be on center stage to make it clear how heroic the two of us have been—our desire has always been to show what God can do. What He continues to do every day.

I loved the affirmation we were receiving, yet I still

choked up when I got to the part about reuniting with Heath. For a moment I almost lost it.

We eventually reached the end where our daughters and their husbands each introduced themselves just as anybody else might in Celebrate Recovery, sharing how they were grateful believers in Christ and listing their hurt, hang-up, or habit, then sharing their name.

"My name is Cherry."

"My name is Josh."

"My name is Callie."

"My name is Jacob."

I knew what was coming and couldn't help smiling.

"And now I want to introduce to you the youth minister at our church."

For a moment, the audience sat there wondering why we were suddenly introducing our youth minister right now. Nobody had a clue who else was on stage with us. He walked toward us with the same mischievous grin his father had the first time I saw him.

"This is Heath, our son, the one God gave back to us."

The room suddenly went crazy. Everybody stood up and applauded and cheered as Heath came to the stage in disbelief. Heath, a jokester like his father, shook his head and spoke into the microphone.

"You people are crazy," he joked before introducing himself.

I saw Mac pat Heath on the shoulder and smile, then take off his glasses for a moment and wipe away the tears.

Exceedingly more. More than I could ask for or imagine.

49

SOMETIMES YOU CAN'T MAKE IT ON YOUR OWN

LIFE isn't always going to be blissful and beautiful. You're not always going to be standing in the spotlight at some summit in your life, all smiles and sunshine.

Mary and I were awakened one October night by a phone call from neighbors living down the road, Jason and Missy Robertson. Missy had seen a fire from their window. We jumped up and looked out our bedroom window, and sure enough the back of the shop was engulfed in flames. We ran out of the house while calling 911.

I quickly reached the shop and tried to see if I could save anything. As soon as I opened the shop door, black smoke billowed out. I went in there even though I could hear Mary screaming out my name behind me. Once inside, I couldn't see a thing. All I could get was a shotgun I felt in the corner. I came out coughing, my eyes burning.

Firefighters showed up soon and made us move way back over to the far side of the house. I watched the flames with frustration and concern. Soon we heard propane bottles exploding, along with shotgun and rifle shells. It sounded like a war zone, and flames were shooting a hundred feet in the air. Mary and I held each other and prayed the flames wouldn't jump over to our house. Thankfully the firemen kept that from happening.

Little by little, people heard about the fire and started to arrive. One person had seen the flames from several miles away across the lake. Soon our driveway was full of cars, and a crowd of church family stood in the yard with us, holding our hands as we watched the horrible sight. Phil and Kay Robertson were among the people comforting us that night.

Everything I had worked to build for the past twenty-seven years—all the tools I had collected and maintained for even longer—was now gone, destroyed in flames. But I was just praying that the firemen and our home would be safe.

Even after the firemen saw that the shop was a lost cause and nothing was left worth salvaging, they kept hosing the American flag that was flying next to the shop. The next morning it was still flying in the air while everything else had gone up in smoke.

Fire investigators eventually came for insurance purposes and said the fire was caused by wood rats chewing through electrical wires in the ceiling. The original shop, made out of wood, had gone up in flames like a matchbox.

The Sunday after the fire, we arrived at church emotionally exhausted from looking at the devastation of our yard with the shop sitting in ashes. Decades of work, gone like that in a brilliant burst of flames.

Our preacher, Stan Webb, called us to the front. We stood there in front of everybody, assuming they were going to pray over us. Then all of the sudden the church started singing "God Is Love," and a parade of people started walking down the center aisle toward us.

Every one of them held a tool in their hands.

This included Jesse, a child who wasn't expected to live past a couple of months old but was now ten. He was being pushed by his father in a wheelchair. Jesse couldn't even feed himself, but he was holding a tool for us.

The group included Charlie, crippled from a diving accident and walking with a cane.

All our brothers and sisters were walking down the aisle, placing a mountain of tools in front of us and then hugging us. Our knees were weak and our eyes wet from the flood of love sweeping over our souls. Mary had to sit down on the steps for a moment, overcome with emotion.

A couple who had just placed membership to our church came up afterward to hug us and say, "Man, you guys are really loved here!"

The question isn't whether bad things will come your way, nor is it when they will arrive. The question is this: what am I going to do when the bad times show up on my door-step with their roaring flames?

There have been many times in the past when we weren't sure how we'd pay our bills. Even though the shop was "just stuff," it was valuable equipment and our livelihood that we had accumulated over thirty years. Many old tools could never be replaced. It took a year to build a new shop and get it into operation, and another year to build back our business. In the early 2000s during the recession, we suffered another financial setback. At the time we had two kids in college and were paying for three weddings.

During these times it would have been easy to resort to my old ways, to become the old Mac again. But instead Mary and I relied on God, knowing He was watching over us day and night.

He never stops, either. Not for one second.

50

HOW AM I SUPPOSED TO LIVE WITHOUT YOU?

WHEN God spoke to me in a clear voice as I drove over Cheniere Dam to see Mac in rehab, I remember thinking, *There's no way I'm going to tell our story.*

When Mac got out of rehab, I remember having similar feelings. *I'm not going to AA meetings with Mac and singing "Kumbaya" and "It Is Well with My Soul."*

It took me a while to go to meetings with him. Then I started to attend, but for the first year I didn't say one single word. I still thought Mac was the messed-up one and I had all my stuff together. I just wanted to forget about the past and move forward with the love of my life, who was sober now and high on Jesus.

Growing up the middle child, I learned to be a people pleaser and a peacemaker. I wanted everybody to like me. When we got married, I took it up a notch and wore myself out keeping secrets and trying to uphold the perfect-little-family look. I made excuses for Mac's behavior, for the times he didn't show up for church or the girls' events. I did anything and everything any church member or schoolteacher asked. I never said no to anybody's requests. Their emergencies took precedence over my own emergencies.

I had no boundaries. I thought if I did enough good things and didn't displease anyone, then I was a good Christian. At times I was exhausted from the turmoil going on in my own life, but I sure wasn't going to tell anyone.

All along I thought it was my job to make sure Mac stayed straight, not realizing he needed to make his own choices and suffer the consequences. That was confusing to me at times, because I thought being a Christian meant saving others from themselves. I didn't realize I had control issues. But at Al-Anon, which I attended while Mac was in AA, I started learning about something called codependency...

In the first years of recovery, I would be distraught when friends would go back out into the world, back to their old hurts and habits. I thought if I just did enough for them, that wouldn't happen. I felt it was somehow my fault when they relapsed.

During my first Celebrate Recovery Step Study, answering the questions in the guidebook really brought my codependency to light. But laughter always helps, and here are some jokes Mac likes to tell at the One Day CR seminars. If you have some of the same issues I struggle with, you may identify.

1. You know you're codependent when you get kicked off jury duty for insisting that you're the guilty one.
2. You're codependent for sure if, when you die, someone else's life flashes in front of your eyes.
3. Q: What do you call a codependent who says no and doesn't feel guilty?

   A: Cured
4. Q: Why did the codependent cross the road?

   A: To help the chicken make a decision.
5. Did you hear about the codependent who flunked geography? He couldn't distinguish any boundaries.
6. You know you're codependent if you find yourself in a rut—and move in furniture.
7. You're codependent for sure when you wake up in the morning and say to your mate: "Good morning, how am I?"
8. Q: Why does a codependent buy two copies of every self-help book?

   A: One to read and one to pass on to someone who really needs it.
9. Q: What does a codependent have in common with God?

   A: They both have a plan for your life.

At Celebrate Recovery I learned to truly deal with my codependency issues.

Back when Mac was still active in his addictions, I took responsibility for other's behaviors. Now I allow others to make their own choices.

Back then I felt guilty about others' feelings. I worried about how they might respond to my opinions, and feared being rejected. Now I get my self-worth from Christ.

Back then I put others' needs above my own, including the need to serve and perform. Now I serve because I'm grateful for what God has done in my life, and not for affirmation.

Back then I felt I could never do enough and felt it was *my* job to take care of others, especially those in recovery. Now I allow God to work in people's lives. It's not up to me to make them see what I see. If they want to hear it, I will share what God has done for me. I plant the seed and then let God water and nurture it.

For a while in my life I had allowed Satan to turn that strength of mine—caring for others and wanting to encourage them—into a weakness. But after getting healthy in recovery, I've now been able to give hope to other women who have similar struggles.

In 2009 I became the National Encourager Coach for women in Celebrate Recovery. Me—the same person who had told God, "No thanks" regarding sharing our testimony, the same person who always let people run over me and who tried to please everybody I could out there.

I never would have imagined becoming a leader in CR. Nor could I ever have imagined telling our story in book form for the whole world to see.

51

HEY YOU

I barely recognize him. The man moving at a hundred miles a minute, all skin and bones, with a raging fire in his soul. I walk toward this twenty-nine-year-old husband and father working in his woodshop.

I turn off the stereo cranking Pink Floyd and see him glance my way. I wonder if I look old to him, because I know he feels like the oldest man in the world, with a racing heart that's on the verge of blowing up any second.

"Hey, Mac," I tell him.

He gives me his suspicious, superior look. I know it masks a soul full of fears.

"You're hard at work."

He nods.

"You know it's three in the morning, right?"

He doesn't know this; he doesn't care.

"Can we sit down and talk?"

This isn't really happening, of course. And I don't really like remembering that guy, because he's a stranger. But he's a part of me, a part I can never forget. And if I could go back in time and tell him what I know now, this is what I would say.

I want to tell him to stop. Not just using drugs, but running from God.

I want to tell him he'll never, ever be able to outrun Him. I want to tell him it's stupid to even try.

I want to say it gets better. After a lot of hard work and a lot of tears and a lot of heartache.

I want to tell him the hurt doesn't go away, not fully, but I also want to tell him that it's what we do with the hurt that matters.

"You can matter," I want to tell him. "You can mean something."

I want to tell him that Jesus is more than a carol at Christmas and an egg on Easter. That this Jesus Christ gave up every awesome thing He had to come into this awful world and save a sinner just like Mac. Some guy destroying himself and destroying every good thing around him. Jesus gave His life and His breath to die for the mistakes this guy is making and will continue to make.

"But it's okay. Because He loves you. He loved you when you were first formed and He loves you in all your faults and He will continue to love you until your final breath."

I want to tell him it gets better. Because, brother, it does. It does.

I want to shake him and shove some sense into his soul.

But mostly I just want to hug him and tell him to stop being so scared. To let go. To know there's more to this life.

"There's a purpose in the pain you're wading around in, Mac."

I want to tell him that same fire inside can be used for the Lord.

I want to tell him that purpose is going to shine and keep shining. He's going to shine like some crazy, recovering diamond.

I want to say all this, but I can't.

I just know that, in time, with God's help and a host of godly men and women, and through the gifts and talents and love from so many of "those people," this guy is going to get it.

This solitary figure in his shop in the middle of the night will always be there to haunt me. But God is stronger than those shadows. His light always shines through.

February 22, 2013. It was twenty-five years.

Twenty-five years of being a grateful believer who still struggles and will continue to struggle until I will struggle no more when Jesus returns (Philippians 1:6).

Thank You, Jesus, for loving the me I used to be, the me I wouldn't have loved, the me I would've let go.

You never let go.

Never.

52

LOVE IS WAR

February 26, 2013

Mac,

When we first met, I never imagined in my wildest dreams that I would spend the rest of my life with you. We were only fourteen and fifteen years old. But that one hello has turned into forty years now. It's been one adventure after another. From waking up under a star-filled sky in sleeping bags with snow in our hair to paddling down Class 5 rivers. Remember the day I followed you jumping off that hundred-foot cliff into the water at Heber Springs? We lived out Survivor *in real life before there ever was such a show.*

But the most exciting adventure of all was when you said, "I'm giving my life to Christ. I can't do this anymore on my own." I actually thought our adventures were going to slow down and we would live a nice calm little family life. But God had a much bigger plan for us than just taking care of ourselves. We saw Him start to weave together a plan of helping others find the hope we had found.

John and Cheryl Baker were healing in their recovery at the same time we were. God was working in both of our families' lives for the next sixteen years before He would bring our paths together. He had planted a seed in all of our hearts of helping others find healing through recovery. And God has been growing it one step at a time, one day at a time, one person at a time.

When I think about you, I think about this verse: "Now the Lord is the Spirit, and where the Spirit of the Lord is, there is freedom." When I think about you and the freedom that you have now from those addictions, I think of this: "And we all, who with unveiled faces contemplate the Lord's glory, are being transformed into His image with ever-increasing glory, which comes from the Lord, who is the Spirit" (2 Corinthians 3:18).

That's what I see now looking at you, Mac. When we tell those old stories, I feel almost like we're talking about someone else, somebody I don't even know anymore because it's so far removed.

When I look at you now, I just see you transformed. And it just gets better and better. Just this ever-increasing glory, which comes from the Lord.

Every time I look at you, I see this man I never could have imagined, though I hoped and believed he was down there all along. I knew there was a good man inside of you. It's just he got lost for a while.

Mac, I can't imagine ever doing anything else than what we are doing right now until Jesus returns or He takes us home. I am right by your side, ready to continue sharing what God has done, is doing, and what He will do as we continue to submit our lives and our wills over to His care.

Love,

Mary

March 1, 2013

Mary,

I will never forget the first day I really saw you, a good-looking fifteen-year-old hippie chick wearing the coolest clothes. Yeah, I'd seen you before at church, but that didn't count, because there you were just another "church girl." But when I saw you in the hallway, I thought, "Wow, that girl is cool. I want to get to know her. I can't believe she goes to church."

Well, it would be a couple of months before I got the chance to go out with you that night after camp. Since that night we have been inseparable. I knew from the very beginning that there was something special about you, something I'd never seen in another girl and for that matter something I've never seen in another woman to this very day. You are the one that God made to complete me.

Oh yeah, there've been plenty of stormy times, but there've been a lot of great times too. The first ten years started out so exciting and fun, only to end up in a place neither of us imagined we would be. And that ten-year period ended in another hallway, this time watching you walk out of my life, hoping I would "get better." I'll never forget that day as I watched your back from behind those closed doors, still able to hear every footstep as you walked away from me. That scene plays over and over in my mind even now, twenty-five years later. Because that was the day I had something to prove. I had to prove I could be the man God wanted me to be. Oh yeah, I wanted to be better for me, but more than that, I didn't want to lose the love that you so graciously poured out on me when I wasn't the man God intended me to be. That marked the most significant change in my life to this day. That was the day I would start to win your love back.

You gave me a Bible at the start of that journey with my name printed on the outside and Psalm 18 marked on the inside. You made it clear that to win you back, I needed to run after God and build a relationship with Him that I'd never had. You know what? It worked. The more I fell in love with God, the more you fell in love with me and the more I idolized every glance you would give me.

Our life was literally a whirlwind, growing deeper in love with God and with each other every day. It's really hard to describe the next ten years of our lives. There were people in our home daily. We were going to meetings nightly and church every chance we got. We would never miss an opportunity to be around good godly people, but the cool thing was we were doing it together. From the very first day God put mentors in our life who would help us in this new walk we were on. Like Ray and Sharon Melton, Bill and Margaret Smith, Phil and Kay Robertson, and of course your dad. He believed in me when it seemed almost no one else did.

Some people might think, "Well, the adventurous life you'd lived before is over now, right?" And of course the answer to that would be, "Not hardly!" It really had just begun. When I came home and told you, "Mary, we need to start our own group to help people like us," you didn't say things like "No, we don't need to do that," or "We're doing just fine on our own now." Instead you were right there with me as we presented our idea to help hurting people to all the elders of our church. You were right beside me every time I would say, "Hey, there's a hurting couple here; let's have them in our home for a meal." You never balked when I would bring home somebody looking really rough because they just needed help. You treated all the strays that I brought home like they were future family members.

Mary, in short, you've always believed in me. You believed in me when I was at my worst. You thought I could get better. You believed in me as a new Christian. That I would step up and become the spiritual leader of our home. And now as we grow old together, you still believe in me as we move into the next adventure.

What I'm really trying to say is thanks for never letting go.

Love,

Mac

53

STAIRWAY TO HEAVEN

EACH *of us has our own song*. These were the words written by Mary's dad in his book *Morsels for the Road.* And it's true. Everybody has his or her own unique song, and nobody else can sing it but you.

Yet for many years I let others sing out my song. The songs had one continual theme: good times. The lyrics had one simple message: party. But those songs were all about me. They were selfish and very unsatisfying. They were stuck in the past with no thought of a God above or an eternity to follow.

One day my little daughter put a mirror up in front of my face and allowed me to see what I was doing to her. To our family. God allowed that girl to come alongside me and break my heart. In doing so, God saved my heart and soul.

My song for today is from Psalm 98:1. I'm singing a new song to the Lord for every wonderful deed He's done. His hand waves the victory flag, and His holy arm rises to show His saving grace.

I'm singing a new song.

Sure, the broken pieces and the messy parts are all still there. They're just stitched and patched over like those cool jeans Mary used to wear. I'm still a work in progress, still wanting to do it my way, still daily humbled by God's grace and mercy. The difference is I'm singing a new song now.

Those old songs will always mean something to me because they're part of my history. They are like the scars on my body. Self-inflicted in pursuit of pleasure. But they will no longer define me.

Your song can change. The song *doesn't* have to remain the same. That's the amazing and cool and awesome part of Christ's love. It'll make you sing a joyful new song. It can still be loud and rocking, but its message will change. So will your life. So will your outlook.

Don't think it's possible?

Really?

Take a look at the men and women God chose to use, the ones who are specifically highlighted in the Bible.

God only uses broken people. All of God's great leaders were broken.

And all of God's great leaders were in recovery.

Abraham, in recovery for lying and not trusting God. He became the father of all those who are faithful, because of his great faith.

Moses, who had a problem with anger. Every time he got angry, he hit something and broke it. God would choose him to lead the largest exodus of God's people ever. And do some of the greatest miracles, which even nonreligious people talk about.

Then there was David, who struggled with purity issues. He's the kind of man we wouldn't allow to be alone with his computer unless his accountability partners were in the room with him. He became someone God described as "a man after my own heart."

Then there was Paul, who was so distracted with religion that he justified killing God's people. He would later tell the believers that before he was a Christian, he came from the right family, the right tribe, the right city. He went to the right schools; he was taught by the right teachers. He was legalistically faultless. Then when he became a Christian, he would say, "I don't know why I can't do the right things. I know what they are but I seem to always want to do wrong. Oh, what a wretched man I am. It's only because of Jesus Christ I am saved today." Then God would say, "Because you are that broken man, I'm going to use you to write down two-thirds of the New Testament and call the Gentiles home where they belong."

Then there's Peter, an ordinary fisherman who struggled with anger and abandonment issues. He would be used in an incredible way. God chose this man who had turned his back on his friend and God's Son to take the first gospel message to thousands of people. And because of Peter's willingness to surrender to God's will, three thousand people responded to the message that day. And Peter was sold out enough to think, *You know what? Let's just baptize them all right now!* And that's exactly what they did.

And it wouldn't be fair if I didn't mention some of the great godly women in the Bible that God also called. Women like Mary Magdalene, who had so many demons they didn't even name them all. And then Jesus would choose her to be the first one He appeared to in His resurrected body. An angel gave her a message: "Go tell Peter and the other apostles that I'm back!"

And then there was Rahab; you remember her? She was self-employed. A woman that many of us today would not give a second chance. God not only used her to hold the safety of His people in her hands, but she also shows up somewhere pretty incredible: in the lineage of His Son!

That's just a short list of broken people God chose to change the world.

Jesus' first words in the Beatitudes are "Blessed are those who are spiritually poor." In other words, "If you're not broken, I got nothing for ya."

54

BETTER IS ONE DAY

ALMOST twenty years ago I wrote this in my journal:

I always hoped Heath's eighteenth birthday would be the time we would meet our son. That milestone has occurred, and I still don't know when it will be, if ever. Someone encouraged me yesterday with the thought "God is never late." This really touched me deeply. I must always remember this. He has the best planned for Mac, me, the girls, and Heath.

Please forgive me, Lord, for trying to figure everything out. I realize now, I cannot. I leave it totally in Your hands.

I feel like I've had a dark cloud over my head about this for eighteen years. But I know there is a silver lining among the dark clouds. God is preparing me for better things to come.

I anticipate the future with excitement. My little mustard seed of faith has grown so much as I can see what God has done and is doing in my life.

Psalm 34:18—"The LORD is close to the brokenhearted and saves those who are crushed in spirit."

He has His arms around me. He loves me so much!

At the time I didn't know whether God would ever answer those prayers of mine. I've learned sometimes He says yes, sometimes no, sometimes later, and sometimes greater. I just had to give all my concerns to Him. Give them to Him and trust.

Do you ache? Do you have a dark cloud over your head?

Know this.

God knows, and God has a plan.

Back in the darkest days of my life, I looked up and saw this oppressive storm that refused to move. I trusted and prayed and believed that God knew and that He had a plan. Then I waited. I thought it might not happen until heaven, but I still waited.

Then it happened, way before I expected it too.

Sometimes it doesn't get better until heaven. I've seen that happen with some people. They still were in trouble when they left here and went on to the Lord without seeing all the change they prayed for.

If I could encourage you in your journey today, know this: it's going to be okay in the end. For all of us who believe in Him.

God won't waste your hurts, if you will just let Him continue to work in your life.

53

FREE BIRD

SO this is what it's like to be a son of the King.

There's freedom. There's grace. And there's love.

If I leave here tomorrow, I know where I'm headed.

But if I stay here, I know there are still things to be done. Places to go and people to meet and stories to be told.

Yeah, I'm free as a bird, but this bird was changed. This bird was broken and nearly beaten to death, but the Lord knew and the Lord changed me. He broke me, then set me free.

This is what it's like to be a son of the King. There's still heartache and still pain. I'm still that flawed Mac and always will be.

But the Lord knows. He helps out. He doesn't define me by my past hurts, by my pesky hang-ups, and by my pathetic habits.

The Lord knew I could change.

He's set me free like a bird, the songs in my soul and the freedom in my heart.

I didn't do any of this. But I did ask for His help. And it came. By God's grace, help arrived.

Help continues to arrive day after day.

This is the rocky road, the one with lots of peaks and valleys, the one with no clear and straight line. It's the only true road to recovery.

I'm not the one in control on this road. In and of myself my life is always—*always*—going to be unmanageable.

But happy are those who know they are spiritually poor.

I gotta know with every ounce of my being and every fiber in my bones that God is real. That HE IS REAL and that somehow, in some way, He loves me. I matter to Him the same way a child matters to his parent. I can't do life on my own. But God? God can do anything. He can help me recover if I will let Him.

'Cause happy are those who mourn, for they shall be comforted.

I have to—HAVE TO—give my thoughts and plans and will over to Christ's care and control. Then, and only then, can I relish this thought:

Happy are the meek.

I need to study my faults. I need to examine them like a chemistry project and then confess them like a convicted criminal to myself and to God and to someone else. Then, and only then, can I relax and know this thought:

Happy are the pure in the heart.

I have to sign up for PROJECT CHANGE. Any and all transformations God wants to make in my life have to be done. I need to stay humble. I need to keep asking God to remove all those defects.

'Cause happy are those whose greatest desire is to do what God requires.

I have to evaluate all the relationships I have in my life. I need to offer forgiveness to those who have hurt me. And believe me—that's not easy. But I also have to make amends for the harm I've done to others when I'm able to, as long as it doesn't harm them or others.

'Cause happy are the merciful. And happy are the peacemakers.

God deserves my time, and I need to make time for Him. To continue to examine my dreadful, sorry self. To read from the Bible even if I think I have it memorized. To pray constantly. I need to do this to know God and His will for me. And not just that, but to gain the power to follow that will.

Then I need to make sure God can use me to bring all of this really, really good news to others. By the things I say and the things I do. And hopefully by then, I'll know this:

Happy are those who are persecuted because they do what God requires.

This isn't some self-help guru's recovery program. This is God's recovery program. All of these guidelines are ways of making your life and making *you* happy. Not forced and not imprisoned and not bored and not miserable, but happy.

This is how you celebrate recovery. It's not a brand and not a box, but it's God's lessons to all of those who have hurts, hang-ups, and habits. Which, last time I looked, was everybody. First and foremost, starting with me.

56

YOU NEVER LET GO

NEVER let go of hope. Never think that freedom is out of your reach. *The Lord is the Spirit, and where the Spirit of the Lord is, there is freedom.*

Whenever I see that mischievous, sly grin on Mac's face, I think of this verse. I think of God taking and breaking this man before me. I think how now I continue to see him being transformed into God's image with an ever-increasing glory. A glory that only comes from the Lord—not from Mac and not from Celebrate Recovery and definitely not from me, but only from the Lord who is the Spirit.

Never let go of one another. Never stand alone and never let others be isolated.

God is the Father of compassion and the God of all comfort. He comforts us in our troubles, so in that same way we should comfort those in trouble themselves. Comfort them with that same comfort we receive from God.

Never let go of your dreams. Never think God is too big for them, that His plan is insufficient for them.

And never, ever let go of God.

Never forget that these troubles are just light and momentary. They're going to achieve for us an eternal glory that far outweighs them all.

"So we fix our eyes not on what is seen, but on what is unseen, since what is seen is temporary, but what is unseen is eternal."

That's how it once was for me and for Mac. It looked like this huge storm that was never going to go away.

But God had a plan. He had a plan all along, plans for good for our family.

He continues to have plans for us, and He has plans for you.

Never let go of these things. Never let go of God. Never let go.

EPILOGUE

IT is March 15, 2013, and we have all our grandkids with us: Caroline, Gannon, Jett, Owen, Solomon, Anna Kate, Silar, and Sayla-Jewell—plus Rex and Summit, who Cherry and Callie are carrying and whose due dates are just one day apart. God's blessings and His sense of humor continue to shower down upon our family.

Mac and I are wondering if this is a sign to open up a day care.

Joking aside, we have been blessed to have undergone a major transition in our lives.

Mac has always wanted to live in Colorado. We used to vacation there with the kids, and as we were leaving, Mac would always say the same thing: "My chest feels so heavy.

I feel like we are supposed to live in those mountains." But I would always say no, we have to live by family. Don't even think it!

Then we met Heath and took him, his mother, and grandmother to Colorado on a vacation. It got in Heath's blood too. Three years ago Heath moved his family to the Centennial State.

After much praying, I eventually realized the truth.

"I'm ready to move to Colorado if you are."

"Don't mess with me," Mac said in disbelief. "Are you serious?"

So we started praying for a year not to get ahead of God. Gradually we felt more and more like the timing was right for us to move. Then our son-in-law Jacob was accepted into the Colorado School of Mines (engineering school). So we put our house on the market and started looking for mountain land.

For a while there were no bites on selling our Louisiana house. We couldn't find the right land in Colorado, either. It was either too expensive or in the city. We began to wonder if God really wanted us to move, but we just kept doing the next right thing in front of us and praying about it.

A few days before the Celebrate Recovery Summit in August 2012, our other son-in-law, Josh, said he wanted to buy our home and turn it into a recovery house. He had already been to the bank to talk to his friend Ben Jones.

"We want to loan you the money for this," Ben had told him. "We know this is a good thing and we want to be involved."

Two days later we got a call from Vicki, our Colorado Realtor. We had told her six months earlier we didn't want to look anymore until we sold our house, but she wanted us to know that a piece of property we liked had become available.

Coincidence? I say it's a God-incidence!

So after the Summit we flew to Colorado to look at the land. When we got there, Vicki's associate, Raeann, said that another property had just come on the market a week before, and we might be interested. When we saw it, we knew it was the one.

We feel God is loaning us a piece of heaven on earth!

As we left our house in West Monroe, we thought about all the memories tied to this one place. We worked hard on this land, played hard, partied hard, worshipped hard, laughed hard, and cried hard there. And now recovery will continue there.

God was there throughout it all, watching over us, extending His hand with grace and mercy. I could see my dad with Jesus right then, knowing they were smiling as they saw the big picture—something we can't see fully until His return.

Right before we left, fifteen guys were sitting in our den at six in the morning, ready for Bible study.

Mac and I had never imagined in our wildest dreams that God would use the house where we found recovery as a haven for others on a similar road. Over the course of twenty-five years, so many would come through those doors to find hope for themselves and begin their own recovery journey. We are so grateful that the legacy continues; there is now a group of eighteen men living in our Louisiana house, finding healing and being reunited with their families. The same God who performed such amazing miracles in the Bible is still doing it today.

When all the families were here sitting on the church pew last March, I looked at Callie and Cherry sitting next to their father with Heath nearby. I thought how it was when they were young: our two little girls next to us, and the memory of Heath in our hearts and minds. Sometimes now, with all our grandkids and the whirl and energy of youth, it's difficult to relax and step back to enjoy the moment. But for this moment, I was able to look back and see this beautiful snapshot.

It reminded me of another sweet snapshot and another little girl.

This one watches her father playing the piano, singing along with him as he makes up songs. They laugh, and he puts his arms around her and gives her a warm, reassuring grin. Then he sings a song he creates right there with her at his side.

"Let's call it 'There's a Rainbow in the Cloud.' As a reminder of God's love for us."

Throughout his whole life, my dad believed and taught us that God is always working things together for the good of those who love Him. I'm also thankful that Dad was right. I'm thankful he taught me about Romans 8:28, which I used as a life raft for many years. Many times I didn't know how God could be working in everything, but I continued to believe and trust.

Now I can see all the many ways God works for the good of those who love Him, who have been called according to His purpose.

Mac and I found our purpose when we had nowhere else to turn. When we finally hit rock bottom and could only stare upwards toward an uncertain and cloudy horizon. But we loved Him and tried to trust Him and tried to remember Romans 8:28.

We tried to remember that yes, indeed, there's a rainbow in the cloud.

It's just over twenty-five years to the day another little girl stood by her father, but in a much different way. This girl was demanding to know why he wouldn't get out of bed and go to church with them. She wanted her daddy back.

That seems like a lifetime ago, yet I can remember it like it happened yesterday. It makes my stomach flip-flop, reliving that day. I truly didn't know if I was going to survive the insanity. That's why I needed to remember and keep remembering that God sees the big picture and He is always right on time. It's easy seeing it in hindsight, but when you're in the middle of chaos, that's when holding on to hope is vital.

Maybe you're a friend, or maybe we've never had the pleasure of meeting. Maybe you've been in recovery for longer than we have been, or maybe you picked this book up on a whim. Maybe you're still hurting and our story has only scratched the surface to help you.

All the maybes in the world can't compete with the definitive power of God's grace and love. There are a thousand stories like ours, different but ending the same way: with the healing, hopeful Savior.

This is our story, but it can be your story too.

Regardless of what has happened to you in the past, you can start anew. You can start a new legacy for your family. It's never too late.

We don't want you to remember Mac and Mary, but we want you to remember what Jesus did for us. We want you to know the Father who spared our marriage and our lives and our family. We want you to know the Spirit who breathed in us a new life.

Even though Mac and I found recovery, we still have hurts in our lives. No one is exempt from hurt on this earth.

It's what we do with that hurt that matters.

ACKNOWLEDGMENTS

JOHN the apostle said, "If all the stories had been told about Jesus there wouldn't be enough room for the books that would be written." We feel the same about the many people who at different times in our lives helped shape who we are today. It would take volumes to mention them all by name.

Countless people have helped direct our paths to find the healing grace of our Savior Jesus Christ. We thank God for our family, friends, and fellow allies on this recovery path.

We thank God every time we think of you, and we remember all of you with prayers of joy "because of your partnership in the gospel from the first day until now, being confident of this, that he who began a good work in you will carry it on to completion until the day of Christ Jesus" (Philippians 1:3-6, NIV).

SPECIAL ACKNOWLEDGMENT

SINCE our encounter with God, when He met us right where we were and refused to let us stay there, we've always known we were supposed to tell our story. Whether it was to one person or an audience of thousands, we couldn't silence the hope God gave us.

That's when God brought Travis Thrasher into our lives. While sharing our story at a Celebrate Recovery seminar in 2012, Travis was in the audience. Later that afternoon Travis told us how our story had touched him. And he said, "This story needs to be in a book."

Since that day Travis has become not only our collaborator in writing our story but also a part of our Forever Family. We love his passion giving people hope through his writings. God has gifted him with such an amazing talent of creative writing. We see Travis as one of God's storytellers. There's no doubt in our minds that God has brought our paths together on our recovery journey to share the hope we've found in Jesus Christ.

Everyone has a story to tell. And we thank Travis for putting the pen to our part of God's story.

"So speak encouraging words to one another. Build up hope so you'll all be together in this, no one left out, no one left behind" (I Thessalonians 5:11, The Message).

CELEBRATE RECOVERY

SOME of you who picked this book up find yourself in a place needing healing from your own hurts, hang-ups, and habits. We could not close without letting you know that hope is available. There is a safe place for you to share your life struggles in churches all across the world. There are people waiting at Celebrate Recovery to welcome you into their family and walk alongside you on this journey called life.

Six features that make Celebrate Recovery unique are stated in *Your First Step to Celebrate Recovery* by John Baker.

1. **Celebrate Recovery is based on God's Word, the Bible.** When Jesus taught the Sermon on the Mount, He began by stating eight ways to be happy. Today we call them the Beatitudes. From a conventional viewpoint, most of these statements don't make sense. They sound like contradictions. But when you fully

understand what Jesus is saying, you'll realize that these eight principles are God's road to recovery, wholeness, growth, and spiritual maturity.

2. **Celebrate Recovery is forward looking.** Rather than wallowing in the past or dredging up and rehearsing painful memories over and over, we confront our past and move on. Celebrate Recovery focuses on the future. Regardless of what has already happened, the solution is to start making wise choices now and depend on Christ's power to help us make those changes.

3. **Celebrate Recovery emphasizes personal responsibility.** Instead of playing the "accuse and excuse" game of victimization, this program helps us face up to our own poor choices and deal with what we can do something about. We cannot control all that happens to us, but we can control how we respond. That is a secret of happiness. When we stop wasting time fixing the blame, we have more energy to fix the problem. When we stop hiding our own faults and stop hurling accusations at others, then the healing power of Christ can begin working in our mind, will, and emotions.

4. **Celebrate Recovery emphasizes spiritual commitment to Jesus Christ.** The third principle calls for us to make a total surrender of our lives to Christ. Lasting recovery cannot happen without this principle. Everybody needs Jesus.

5. **Celebrate Recovery utilizes the biblical truth that we need each other in order to grow spiritually and emotionally.** It is built around small group interaction and the fellowship of a caring community. There are many therapies, growth programs, and counselors today that operate around one-to-one interaction. But Celebrate Recovery is built on the New Testament principle that we don't get well by ourselves. We need each other. Fellowship and accountability are two important components of spiritual growth.

6. **Celebrate Recovery addresses all types of hurts, hang-ups, and habits.** Some recovery programs deal only with alcohol or drugs or another single problem. But Celebrate Recovery is a "large umbrella" program under which a limitless number of issues can be dealt with. At Saddleback Church, only one person out of three who attend Celebrate Recovery is dealing with alcohol or drugs. We have many other specialized groups.

Celebrate Recovery is in over twenty thousand churches worldwide. And over one million people have gone through a Celebrate Recovery Step Study. You are not alone. There is hope for healing. Freedom is possible.

www.celebraterecovery.com

TO CONNECT

www.macandmaryowen.com

www.travisthrasher.com

BE A TOTEM POLE!